Please renew or return items by the date shown on your receipt

www.hertfordshire.gov.uk/libraries

Renewals and enquiries: 0300 123 4049

Textphone for hearing or 0300 123 4041
speech impaired users:

L32 11.16

D1422707

525 545 93 0

The Countryside Year

THE COUNTRYSIDE YEAR

Summersdale Publishers Ltd
46 West Street
Chichester
West Sussex
PO19 1RP
UK

www.summersdale.com

Printed and bound in the Czech Republic

ISBN: 978-1-84953-683-7

Substantial discounts on bulk quantities of Summersdale books are available to corporations, professional associations and other organisations. For details contact Nicky Douglas by telephone: +44 (0) 1243 756902, fax: +44 (0) 1243 786300 or email: nicky@summersdale.com.

The Countryside Year

Steve Barnett

summersdale

January

Country things are the necessary
root of our life.

Esther Meynell

MIDWINTER. FROSTS, SNOW, *bare trees. The rhythm of
life has slowed: many of the countryside's animal
inhabitants are hibernating while migratory birds
have headed south, reducing the number of birds to
be seen. Farmers in many parts have taken cattle and
other stock into barns. But the days are lengthening
and life is starting to stir. On the tilled ground of the
farmers' fields, the first green threads of winter wheat
may be seen.*

Wildlife

MANY OF NATURE'S animals continue in their long winter sleeps, passing this hard season when sources of food are at best scarce, if not absent. A redoubtable winter sleeper is the dormouse, whose very name – from the French word '*dormer*', meaning 'to sleep' – is a nod to its great sleeping ability. In the dense nest it has built inside a tree cavity or similar sheltered place, the dormouse sleeps away the months from September through April. In order to conserve energy this little creature slows down its metabolism during these months by a remarkable 90 per cent.

ONCE COMMON IN the countryside, the dormouse – or hazel dormouse as it is also known – is now rarely seen. It makes its home in deciduous woodland and hedgerows. Here it seeks out berries, hazelnuts and insects. Travelling along branches and thickets, dormice can spend long parts of their lives without ever touching the ground. The dormouse is one of many countryside creatures severely affected by loss of habitat and modern farming practices.

OTHER WINTER SLEEPERS are the amphibians; frogs, toads and newts. Frogs and toads hibernate in burrows in muddy ground and at the bottom of ponds. Newts will find somewhere sheltered on land or hibernate in the mud at the bottom of ponds.

January

THE NATTERJACK TOAD, common frog, edible frog, common toad, and marsh frog are among the amphibians most frequently seen. Apart from the size difference – toads are usually larger – toads are differentiated by having drier, wartier skin: frogs' skin is smoother. If you come across spawn in a pond, remember that toad spawn appears in strings, while frogs lay their eggs in clumps.

THE THREE NEWT species native to Britain spend most of their time on land, returning to ponds and streams just to breed. They are lizard-like, although their skin is smooth compared to the scaly skins of lizards. As with all newts, the palmate newt, the smooth newt and the great crested or warty newt (the most common of the three) have the ability to regrow limbs lost in accidents or to predators.

ONE OF THE features of Britain's birdlife is the diversity it gains by way of migrant, summer-breeding species and also visiting overwintering species – January may be cold in Britain, but it is much colder in northern Europe, from where the latter wing their way here. One such winter visitor is the siskin: a small, lively finch which joins resident siskins found from the south of England through to the top of Scotland.

ANOTHER WINTER VISITOR to Scotland and north-east England is the snow bunting. The British breeding population is very small, estimated at fewer than 100 breeding pairs, while the visiting birds from Arctic Europe arrive in their thousands.
Better known of the buntings group of birds is the yellowhammer, common to farmland, heaths and hedgerows.

Field and Flower

RARE AMONG THE countryside's deciduous trees is the black poplar. Unlike other poplars in the landscape, such as the aspen and Lombardy poplar, the native black poplar requires a constantly damp soil for natural regeneration – an environment that is increasingly unavailable as agricultural lands are drained. A programme of re-establishment of the species is underway with new plantings in river valleys and wetlands in Sussex.

FLOWERS MIGHT BE the last thing you expect to encounter during the cold climes of winter. Look closely, however, and you'll discover one of the most romantic of all winter wildflowers: the much-loved common snowdrop, generally considered to be the first flower of the year. Damp woodland, shady churchyards, banks and verges are its home.

THE HAZEL, OR cobnut, may appear a sombre tree to some at this time; its drooping catkins frozen still in the winter air. Its fruit, cobnuts, are a favourite of squirrels. Similar to hornbeam, hazel is common in hedgerows where its nuts are eaten by dormice looking to fatten up ahead of hibernating.

ANOTHER SO-CALLED WEED that, upon closer inspection, is really quite pretty, is the white dead-nettle or white archangel. Unlike its cousin the stinging nettle, the white dead-nettle doesn't irritate the skin. Its flowers, which can appear as early as this month in mild winters, are whorls of furry white petals, nestled below its various sets of jagged leaves. Look for it in woodlands and at the sides of roads and footpaths.

ANOTHER SPLASH OF winter colour is provided by the Dutch crocus, its purple or yellow flowers are a harbinger of spring. Tennyson likened its orange-yellow flowers to fire.

THERE ARE THOUGHT to be more sheep breeds in Britain than in any other country in the world, with some 60 different varieties producing long and short wools that are used to make carpets, cloth and knitwear, and kept for their meat. Until the eighteenth century sheep had been farmed mainly for their wool, but with the coming of the Industrial Revolution meat took on more importance.

THOSE SHEEP TYPES bred to survive the tough conditions of winter include Rough Fell sheep; one of the largest mountain sheep breeds in Britain, extremely hardy, and as such well able to live in the inclement mountainous and hilly moorland of southern Cumbria, Yorkshire and Lancashire. Carrying a thick white fleece, the Rough Fell has a black head and a white patch on the nose. Rams are horned.

ANOTHER ROBUST BREED is the Swaledale sheep, which takes its name from the Swaledale valley in the North Yorkshire Dales. Medium sized with a black face that sports a white stripe over the eyes and a whitish muzzle, they are also found in other hilly and mountainous locations throughout Britain, mostly in Cumbria and County Durham. Ewes and rams both have horns, although rams' horns are larger and more curved.

Landscape and Culture

THE EVOLUTION OF the countryside dates from about 6,000 years ago when the first farmers began clearing the native wildwood to grow crops. By the time of the Roman occupation the countryside had been largely cleared of its ancient woods and the landscape settled into agricultural use.

IN THE FOLLOWING centuries, the Anglo-Saxons emphasised communal land use, with common grazing lands and woodlands. The Normans in their turn responded to a growing demand for food by bringing marginal lands, woodlands and uplands increasingly under the plough and replacing the traditional open-field system with enclosed fields for more efficient management.

THE INDUSTRIAL REVOLUTION in the eighteenth century further transformed the landscape. Mechanisation reduced the number of people working on the land, and an ever-increasing population demanded greater intensification of agriculture. The land enclosures of the eighteenth and nineteenth centuries saw farms being aggregated for greater efficiency and to suit greater use of mechanisation.

THROUGHOUT THE TWENTIETH century the size of fields continued to grow, which along with the introduction of chemical fertilisers and pesticides ensured higher yields. A consequence has been the huge loss of, and detriment to, wildlife habitat and numbers. Major reductions in populations have been recorded over the last 20 years for birds, mammals, butterflies and other invertebrates and amphibians; in some cases to the point of extinction. The good news is that there is a growing awareness of this threat to Britain's countryside and the public, interest groups and government are active in restoring the countryside, lobbying for reduced chemical use and promoting changes to farming practice.

IN PAST TIMES, shepherds commonly used traditional number systems to count sheep. One such system – a rhyme – used in northern England was 'yan, tan, tethera', or 'one, two, three'. The numbers' names come from an old Gaelic language and the method was based on units of 20. To count a larger number of sheep, the shepherd would mark off each unit by making a mark on the ground or dropping a pebble into his jacket pocket.

SHEPHERDS WERE SOMETIMES buried with tufts of wool in their hands. This was to let St Peter know they were shepherds and that their occupation had prevented them from attending church every Sunday.

Tips

As you walk lanes and tracks in winter, the leafless forms of trees can make identification tricky and observation of the structural aspects that are now revealed is required. Look at tree form and growth habit: how the branches are held, the colour of the bark, the shape of dormant buds and the structure of twigs. With practice you will soon be able to easily identify trees, even at a distance!

Keep in mind that plants in the countryside are protected. It is OK to pick wild fruit, foliage, fungi or flowers, so long as this is for your own use and is not to be sold, but it is illegal to uproot any wild flower without having the permission of the landowner. The countryside is also home to many rare and endangered plants, such as orchids and mosses, which it is against the law to pick.

The beauty of the countryside and its wildlife can be made more enjoyable for many people when they keep a wildlife journal, jotting down the things they've seen and heard and experienced, and perhaps also illustrating the page with sketches (not everyone can draw well, but everyone can sketch!). Keeping such a record will help you hone your observational skills and add to your enjoyment of the countryside.

VISITING BRITAIN'S CANALS and other waterways is
a must. Walking canal or river paths or holidaying
on a narrowboat takes you into the heart of the
countryside, away from the noise of busy roads, and
reveals a rich world of wildlife: newts and frogs,
herons, cormorants and ducks of all kinds, butterflies
and dragonflies, kingfishers, water rats and even otters.
Importantly, the canal system provides corridors
linking up a number of different kinds of habitat
across Britain.

THERE ARE A number of museums around Britain
dedicated to the social history of the countryside,
some of which have 'live' days or working displays.
Three of these are the Dales Countryside Museum in
Hawes (displays include dairying, agriculture and rural
crafts); the Weald and Downland Open Air Museum
in Chichester (set in traditional buildings in a rural
landscape); and the National Museum of Rural Life
near Glasgow (set on a 170-acre historic working farm).

Notes

1
....

2
....

3
....

4
....

5
....

6
....

7
....

8
....

9
....

10
....

11
....

12
....

13
....

14
....

January

15
....

16
....

17
....

18
....

19
....

20
....

21
....

22
....

23
....

24
....

25
....

26
....

27
....

28
....

29
....

30
....

31
....

February

LATE WINTER. LONGER daylight hours are having an effect on fauna and flora – leaf buds are swelling, some birds will start preparations for nesting this month and the first blossoms will appear, cold snaps allowing. Flocks of sheep in sheltered lowlands are lambing and the prospect of new pasture beckons. While trees are still without leaves and such tasks are more easily done, it is a time when some farmers will be planting new woods and coppicing hedgerows.

Wildlife

THE NESTING SEASON in Britain is officially from February until August, but in practice birds may be seen to start gathering material earlier and to continue nesting beyond August. The busiest time is from the beginning of March until the end of July, varying by species. By June many of the young will have left their nests, often making way for a second brood.

'CHAT' IS THE perfectly appropriate collective name for the group of small vocal birds that includes species such as the stonechat, whinchat, robin, wheatear, bluethroat and sweet-singing nightingale. Some are summer residents such as the wheatear, while others, such as the bluethroat, are passing visitors.

THE ROBIN WITH its cheery presence and bright red breast is a favourite, and is especially cherished over wintertime. During winter, resident robins are joined by migrant populations from Europe, mostly from Scandinavia. Robins sing nearly all year round, and will even continue warbling at night in towns – it is thought this is in order to take advantage of the relative quiet so their song can at last be heard! Nests are made using dead leaves, moss and grass which is then lined with wool, perhaps, and strands of hair.

RABBITS AND HARES differ in size – hares are bigger and with larger hind legs – and in the length of their ears – rabbits' ears are shorter. The animals can also be differentiated when they are running, from the way the rabbit raises its tail, displaying a white underside; hares' tails are not raised, and show a black upperside colouring. While rabbits move in groups, the hare tends to be a loner. Both animals feed mainly at dawn and dusk, spending their days laid up in their burrows (rabbits) or in their scrapes on the ground (hares) under cover. Britain is home to a mountain hare that is smaller than the common hare, whose coat turns white in winter as camouflage.

THE BADGER IS one of the icons of the countryside, notable for its size – about 75 cm from head to tail – hefty build and distinctive white head with black stripes over its ears and eyes. The badger's preferred habitat is woodland, especially where this adjoins pastureland. Badgers live in family groups, inhabiting a sett – a complex of chambers and tunnels that may run to 18 m, which they leave after sunset to hunt small mammals, frogs and insects and to feed on berries and windfall fruits. While badgers don't hibernate, they will put on weight at the end of autumn and sleep longer through the winter when food is scarce.

THE WREN IS one of Britain's smallest birds – its size at odds with a loud voice – with an almost rounded form and brown plumage. It gives a distinctive flicking of its tail as it busies itself searching for insects. Highly susceptible to the cold, wrens can often succumb to cold spells and so the birds group together in order to keep warm. Its nest is a domed structure that is built combining leaves, moss and grass.

Field and Flower

EARLY FEBRUARY SEES the emergence of pussywillow; willow stems bearing soft grey, silk-covered catkins. Willow species seen across the countryside include the weeping willow, crack willow and white willow (a form of which supplies the wood used for cricket bats). Goat willow and grey willow (both also known as 'sallow') are the ones whose spring growth we call pussywillow. Goat willow can be found growing in woodland, hedgerows and scrub, and on damper, more open ground such as near lakes, streams and canals.

APTLY NAMED PRIMROSES – 'first rose' – are among the earliest wildflowers to raise their heads in spring. A denizen of woodlands and hedgerows, they do well in shade. Other harbingers of the new season are coltsfoot, whose flowers appear ahead of the leaves, and lesser celandine.

A SMALL PLANT just a few centimetres high, the primrose produces flowers generally varying from a pale cream to deep yellow, although other colour variants, including white and pink, can be seen. Primroses are very much a part of the distinctive character of the countryside in spring, forming wonderful displays on damp and shady hedgebanks and in cool woodland glades. It is similar to the flower of the cowslip, but primrose flowers open flat as opposed to concave in the case of cowslip.

NOW THE HILLS are enlivened and our hearts lifted with the beauty of gorse's golden-yellow flowers, particularly when seen against the clear cold blue of a winter sky. Also called furze, and whin in Scotland, gorse has long been used for farm hedging, the spiky prickly stems an effective deterrent to stock. In addition, gorse thickets provide shelter and food for many of the countryside's birds and insects. There are three species of gorse in Britain, which are all very similar, flowering generally from January to June. The largest and most frequently seen is common gorse; western gorse is lower growing and less widespread while the sprawling dwarf gorse tends to be limited to the heathlands in the south and east. Walk through gorse-covered hills on a hot summer's day and, as with broom, you'll hear the sound of seed pods bursting open from the heat.

THE CATTLE LOWING on Britain's pastures derive from wild stock that traces its ancestry back thousands of years, and that was bred with introduced cattle brought here by the Romans and Anglo-Saxons. Today there are some 20 cattle breeds across dairy, beef and dual-purpose, including famous breeds such as Aberdeen Angus – originally native to Scotland – the Hereford from the Welsh Border counties, and the Highland.

ONE OF BRITAIN'S most distinctive cattle breeds, the Highland, originated in Scotland's Highlands and western coastal islands. Given its ability to survive weather extremes of rain, wind and cold, in a rugged mountainous environment, these are the hardiest of beasts, capable of living from the poorest of grazing. The Highland's double coat of hair – a long outer coat covering a downy under coat – is characteristically russet coloured but can also be brindle, black or dun. Sweeping horns and presence complete the picture!

Landscape and Culture

THE HISTORY OF the system of canals that threads the countryside can be traced back to Roman occupation, but they had their real spur with the Industrial Revolution. The increase in commerce that arose out of the new manufacturing saw canals promoted as a means of transporting raw material to factories, and finished goods to markets, more quickly and with greater capacity than horse and cart. Over the eighteenth and nineteenth centuries more than 4,000 canals and associated waterways were built. But they in their turn were overtaken by the greater efficiency of the railway and many canals fell into abeyance. Today they enjoy a new lease of life with tourism. Narrowboaters appreciate the opportunity to slow-travel through the heart of the countryside at not much more than a walking pace and to be in touch with nature – think *Wind in the Willows* – in a way that is just not possible for those travelling by road.

THE USE OF thatched roofs on houses and farm buildings in the countryside in Britain was commonplace for many hundreds of years until the early 1800s when slate tiles began to be used. Local availability of straw, reeds and broom and their light weight made thatching highly suitable. Wheat straw was favoured in much of Britain; it grew much taller than today – to about 1.8 m – on strong stems that were ideal for use in thatching. This changed in the twentieth century with the advent of hybrid varieties, the demands of machine harvesters and chemical fertilisers which all combined to produce shorter and weaker-stemmed straw. Recent times have seen initiatives for reintroducing the older taller-stemmed varieties especially for thatch as demand increases for more natural and sustainable roofing for countryside buildings and for restoration projects. A good-quality thatch is capable of lasting for at least 50 years.

HERE AND THERE in the countryside one comes across strange and even playful buildings in parks or the grounds of stately homes. Such follies were constructed primarily as decoration and had no practical purpose. They were a fad upheld by wealthy landowners during the eighteenth and nineteenth centuries who were inspired – often following a grand tour of Europe – to enliven their properties with expressions of classical architecture: faux Roman arches, Greek temples and portions of castle walls. 'Folly' is thought to derive from the French '*folie*', meaning 'madness'. '*Folie*' also has an older meaning of 'delight'.

Tips

NIGHT-TIME IN THE countryside reveals a quite different world. Many of the countryside's creatures – such as deer, foxes and badgers – are active at dusk and through the night, and to see them you have to enter their dark world. Before doing so it's an idea to do a daytime recce first to avoid any surprises and to identify places where you can station yourself when it's dark to spot animals – near to a badger sett for instance. Choose dark-coloured clothing for your nocturnal adventure and take along a torch, with a piece of red cellophane held in place with a rubber band over the front of the torch to produce a less invasive light. At night there is a lot less noise. Gradually you'll become accustomed not only to the shapes of fields and trees at night, but also to the different sounds: the scuttle of mice at the bottom of hedgerows, hedgehogs snuffling their way through the field and road margins, the squeaks of certain bats, the calling of ducks or geese perhaps flying high overhead, frogs or the cough of a deer.

FOR THOSE INTERESTED in Britain's follies, there are a number that are open to the public or in public parks. The following three buildings are particularly odd examples of these architectural flights of fancy:

Leith Hill Tower near Dorking in Surrey is a 20-m high Gothic-style tower that was built in the 1760s by Richard Hull who wanted a 'prospect tower' to take in the views of the English Channel and of London. Hull believed that on Judgement Day the world would be turned upside down and so, wanting to ensure he would be the right way up to meet his Maker, he arranged to be buried head down in the base of the tower.

On the other hand, Sir Thomas Tresham's Triangular Lodge (in the grounds of Rushton Hall, near Kettering) was built in the 1590s as a monument to the Holy Trinity – and the number three is at its core. With three storeys, each of the Lodge's three sides measures 33 feet, each side comprising three gables, gargoyles to the power of three and three, yes, triangular windows. Three quotations from the Bible appear on a frieze on the outside walls. Each text consists of, unsurprisingly, 33 letters.

In Dunmore Park in Stirling is the Dunmore Pineapple, a pineapple-shaped cupola atop a garden summer house, built in the 1760s by the Earl of Dunmore. A hothouse on the ground floor was used for growing pineapples, which were incredibly exotic in England at the time. The Pineapple is 14-m high; the summer house is available as holiday accommodation.

Notes

1 ....

2 ....

3 ....

4 ....

5 ....

6 ....

7 ....

8 ....

9 ....

10 ....

11 ....

12 ....

13 ....

14 ....

February

15
....

16
....

17
....

18
....

19
....

20
....

21
....

22
....

23
....

24
....

25
....

26
....

27
....

28
....

29
....

March

EARLY SPRING. DAYBREAK *is earlier and earlier. This month sees the vernal equinox around 20 March so spring is officially here. Woodlands are coming to life. March flowers include common violet, wood anemone, red deadnettle and common fumitory. Hedgehogs and other small mammals are emerging from hibernation. Birds are nest-building. Winter fodder for farm stock kept inside during winter may be running low and farmers will be keen to see signs of fresh grass. In the fields tilling and seed-drilling are underway.*

Wildlife

COMMON ENOUGH IN our cities and towns, the house sparrow is a chirpy and gregarious resident of the countryside as well, seen much of the year moving in flocks across grasslands and through copses. The tree sparrow is distinguished from the common species by its white wing bars, a chocolate-brown crown (rather than grey) and a black patch on its white cheeks. The tree sparrow is less likely to be seen around human habitation, and more likely to be seen in hedgerows and at edges of woodlands.

ALTHOUGH FREQUENTLY CALLED 'hedge sparrow', the dunnock is not in fact a sparrow of any kind. Its pointy bill – that of an insect-eating bird – distinguishes it from the more rounded bills of seed-eating birds, of which the house sparrow is a member. Flitting in and around hedges and tree branches the dunnock is a shy bird with an appropriate dullish brown upper plumage – 'dunnock' comes from ancient British 'dunnakos' meaning 'little brown one'.

BRITISH LADYBIRD SPECIES number about 46, although only half of those are recognisable as classic-looking ladybirds. Many species are named after the number of spots on their wings, but counting these is not always a reliable method of identification – the 13-spot ladybird, for instance, may have up to 15 spots. And some have stripes, patches or streaks. Those you are most likely to see out in the countryside include the 13-spot ladybird, which was once thought extinct in Britain but is these days re-establishing itself; the two-spot ladybird, which in fact can have up to 16 spots and variable ones at that, either black spots (on red) or red spots on black; and the seven-spot ladybird, the species most commonly seen, red with black spots. Newly hatched ladybirds of nearly all kinds are yellow. Only later when the wings harden does the species-specific colouration and marking develop.

THE MOLE SHARES a similar iconic status with the badger and it too is little-seen… given that it spends almost its entire life underground. Only 6-in. long with soft, dark fur, the mole is famously capable of great earth-moving feats in the making of tunnels with its shovel-like, outward turned front limbs and in its search for earthworms, slugs and insect larvae. Molehills are the result of their tunnelling – which can reach up to 20 m a day – and are formed of the excess soil they have pushed to the surface. The mole's vision is poor and is compensated for by highly developed senses of hearing and touch. Its preferred habitat is farmland and grassland, and woodland where soil is friable and sufficiently deep for tunnelling through. The texture of a mole's fur is uniquely uniform and lies readily in any direction, allowing the mole to quickly reverse along a tunnel if need be.

HEDGEHOGS EMERGE FROM hibernation this month. The young – called hoglets – are born from May onwards. Mostly nocturnal, hedgehogs lay up during the daytime under cover of leaf drifts, long grass or beneath hedges until nightfall, when they move off in search of the insects, worms, snails and slugs, windfall fruits and the eggs of ground-nesting birds that make up their diet. Mrs Tiggy-Winkle, the hedgehog washerwoman in Beatrix Potter's famous book *The Tale of Mrs Tiggy-Winkle*, was based on the writer's own pet hedgehog of the same name.

Field and Flower

THE ALDER IS Britain's most common tree, seen along the banks of lakes, rivers and marshes, and is seldom found on drier ground. The near absence of nitrogen in the waterlogged soils in which it roots has produced an unusual adaptation, which means that the alder is able to utilise atmospheric nitrogen instead. Nitrogen-fixing bacteria in root nodules absorb nitrogen from the air and make it available to the tree. In former times in some parts of Britain, charcoal produced from burning alder was a component in making gunpowder.

LIKE THE PRIMROSE, the cowslip is a member of the *Primula* family, but is differentiated from the primrose by the greater height of its flower stalks and the general size of the plant. It also differs in requiring more light in order to flower and is found more on banks and open grassland than the primrose. Delicate yellow flowers open between March and May. Related to the cowslip is the oxlip; it has flowers that are larger than that of the cowslip, and which hang off one side of the flowerhead. (The popular garden polyanthus is also a member of the *Primula* family.)

THE SWEET VIOLET, with its sweetly scented violet (and sometimes white) flowers, is found on woodland margins and on hedgebanks where there is shade and damp. Flowering time is March through to May. Violets were a favourite of the Victorians and bunches of violets were commonly sold by street vendors in villages and towns.

THOUGH ITS APPEARANCE in spring is fleeting, the wood anemone is a lovely star of open deciduous woodland floor and banks. Found in old woodland, it in fact spreads very slowly and is one of the spring flowers of the woodland floor that needs to maximise light coming through the canopy before this leafs over. Starry white flowers often blushed pink rise on tallish stems over whorls of leaves.

AS THE WEATHER warms and the grass comes back, more sheep can be seen on countryside pastures, among them the Cotswold. This is one of the ancient English breeds; they grazed the Cotswold Hills at the time of Caesar's conquest of Britain. A longwool variety, the fleece grows in long braids of wavy curls and by shearing time the animals will have grown a long fringe over their eyes. The name 'Cotswold' is derived from earlier times when sheep were kept in shelters called 'cotes', in 'wolds' meaning hills.

THE LARGEST AND most distinctive of British sheep, the Wensleydale has a bluish-coloured skin and a long curly fleece resembling dreadlocks. This soft fleece produces some of the finest wool in the world. The breed's ancestry can be traced to a specific ram born in 1838 in a hamlet near Bedale in North Yorkshire.

Landscape and Culture

COMMON RIGHTS – that is the rights that Britons have over certain areas of public land – still exist today, with some variation in Scotland. Such rights go back to the Middle Ages when commoners were allowed by the local lord of the manor to avail themselves of the manor's wasteland and its products – to graze stock, collect firewood and take peat. Such rights are known as 'commons'. Later, during the fifteenth and sixteenth centuries, what had been common land began to be enclosed by the lords of the manors for their exclusive use and to enable more efficient farming than that provided by the existing open-field system. In the eighteenth and nineteenth centuries, concurrent with the Industrial Revolution and greater mechanisation of agriculture, enclosure laws enabled even more common land to be transferred to wealthy landowners. Ultimately protests forced an end to further enclosures and remaining common land was preserved for public use.

VILLAGE GREENS WERE usually small parcels of common land close to hamlets and villages where markets were held, stock kept overnight in their droves and the like. Many British villages still retain such greens today, which fulfil many of their traditional uses for sport and markets.

COPPICING IS A very old way of managing woodlands to maximise the usefulness of certain broadleaf trees, by cutting trunks down to near ground level on a repeated basis. This promotes growth of multiple stems from the original stumps. It is a very effective method of producing sustainable timber growth without replanting trees: the existing coppiced trees already have well-developed root systems and regrowth is fast. Interestingly coppicing has the effect of resetting the tree's ageing process, often by hundreds of years. Those species most usually coppiced include oak, field maple, sweet chestnut, hazel ash and willow. Coppicing differs from pollarding in that branches are cut at near ground level, while pollarding cuts at head height or higher.

Tips

PRESSING FLOWERS AND leaves was once a popular pastime – evidence of which is often found when leafing through old books in second-hand bookshops – and is a simple way to preserve flora as a memory of countryside walks; either by way of the tried-and-true method of slipping flowers between book pages, or by using a homemade flower press. It is best to pick flowers or foliage when they are fresh, and wait until any moisture has evaporated naturally before pressing. Place between two sheets of paper – to protect the book pages – before inserting this in-between the book pages. Place some heavy books on top of the book containing the flowers and leave for a few weeks to press flat.

TO MORE FULLY imbibe the flavour of country life, think about renting a countryside cottage for a week or two. There are thousands of cottages available across Britain, or, if you'd prefer, make a long stay at a youth hostel or on a farm stay – or take to the canals in a narrowboat. From such a base you can take time to explore the surrounding countryside by foot or bicycle, go for day hikes, investigate local pubs and more.

LOOK DOWN; LOOK up. When you're out walking, take your time to look both down and up to take in the detail of life on the ground and above your head: the small flowers and herbs on woodland floors and grasslands; birds' nests in trees and quietly hovering kestrels; the movement at the bottom of a hedgerow or road margins that spells the presence of mouse or a shrew; emergent leaf buds; the stars at night.

NIGHT SKIES AWASH with stars are magnificent. Light pollution in towns and cities means that most of us go for years without seeing the glory of a really brightly starred dark sky. It's somewhat easier to experience this in the countryside but more effective if you can target one or other of the darkest places in Britain. Here you can more readily pick out constellations, marvel at the Milky Way and perhaps catch sight of the occasional meteor. Some of the best places to stargaze are: Galloway Forest Park (two hours from Carlisle); Exmoor in Somerset (which has International Dark Sky Reserve status); Romney Marsh in Kent; Kielder Forest in Northumberland (officially the darkest place in England); the North York Moors; Grizedale Forest in the Lake District; Leigh Woods in Bristol; St Agnes and Chapel Porth in Cornwall; Headley Heath in Surrey, and Wicken Fen in Cambridgeshire.

Notes

1
....

2
....

3
....

4
....

5
....

6
....

7
....

8
....

9
....

10
....

11
....

12
....

13
....

14
....

15

16

17

18

19

20

21

22

23

24

25

26

27

28

29

30

31

April

EARLY SPRING. WINDS – in like a lion, out like a lamb – are beginning to calm. Eggshell-blue skies welcome the arrival of many of the summer-breeding migrant birds to Britain, including the first cuckoo. Plants on woodland floors such as forget-me-nots, bluebells and white dead-nettle are taking advantage of warming light to flower ahead of overhead trees coming into leaf. There's new grass now for grazing by cattle that have over-wintered indoors, while in fields grain crops such as oats are putting on growth.

Wildlife

BRITAIN IS HOME to some 250 different types of bee – comprising a couple of dozen bumblebees, more than 200 solitary bees, and just one honeybee species. Most honeybees you'll see in the countryside are from commercial or domestic hives but wild colonies also abound, making their hives for instance in the hollow of a tree. In recent years honeybee populations have been decimated by both the varroa mite and the effect of toxic insecticides.

THE HIVE POPULATIONS of bumblebees are typically much smaller than those of honeybees, at about 30–150 individuals. Compare this with honeybee hives of about 40,000 individuals. Colonies formed by bumblebees last only a single season, at the end of which, in the autumn, all the colony dies off with the exception of the new queens. These hibernate until spring, when they emerge to begin new nests in holes and crevices in the ground.

THE WARBLERS FORM a large group of small, active birds, many of which are resident breeders in Britain, but with summer migrants in some cases swelling the ranks of small resident populations. The warblers comprise a number of groups: leaf warblers – slender and greenish-coloured, found in woodland and scrub; reed warblers – browner plumaged and inhabiting wetter places; and Sylvia warblers – more patterned and, as their group name suggests (as it derives from sylvan), are found in bushy areas and woods. Migrant warblers arrive here in their hundreds of thousands: willow warbler visitors to Britain are said to number about one million.

LIKE OTHER VISITING warblers, the chiffchaff winters in the Mediterranean and in West Africa, and is named for its call of 'chiff-chaff chiff-chaff'. Olive-brown and with an active manner, it flits through trees and shrubs with a distinctive tail-wagging movement. Like many other summer visitors, these migrant warblers take on a flight – usually non-stop – of about 2,000 miles, repeating the trip come autumn.

MORE OFTEN HEARD than seen, the call of the cuckoo traditionally heralds spring, following its arrival from its winter quarters in Africa. The cuckoo famously does not build a nest but fosters out its young instead by laying its eggs (one per nest) in the nests of other birds, who then take over the rearing of the young cuckoo – a fledgling that can be larger than its foster parent! And usually the cuckoo is its new parents' only obligation, given that after hatching out the cuckoo fledgling will usually push the eggs and/or fledglings of the host bird out of the nest.

A RESIDENT OF woodlands and copses, the native red fox hunts by night for small mammals such as mice and rabbits as well as frogs and ground birds. Increasingly foxes also scavenge the outskirts of towns and villages. A smaller animal than many people imagine, the male fox is a bit over 36-in. long including its bushy white-tipped tail, and some 38 cm high.

Field and Flower

MUCH USED IN hedgerows as it sends up suckers which quickly increase the thicket, blackthorn or sloe is a shrubby tree recognisable by its long thorns. White flowers appear on short stalks before the leaves, either singularly or in pairs. The plum-like berries – the tree is an ancestor of the plum – are formed in late autumn and are known as 'sloes'. They are edible but very bitter, and are commonly used in making sloe gin, to which they bring a special flavour.

EARLY BLOSSOM IS provided by the white flowers of wild cherry, short-lived though it is, lasting only a week or two in late April before its confetti-like fall. The wild cherry is perhaps one of our most attractive native woodland trees, often found in old hedgerows and in mixed deciduous woodland, usually at the wood's edge. The shiny bark is reddish-brown lined horizontally with cream lines. The leaves are oval and toothed.

A MEMBER OF the olive family, the ash has dull green leaves that turn pale yellow in the autumn. A magnificent tree in leaf, ash is Britain's third most common tree species after oak and birch. The pinnate structure of ash leaves (multiple leaflets along either side of the main leaf stem), creates an open canopy that prompts a rich variety of plants to grow on the floor beneath, such as beautiful bluebells, wild garlic and dog's mercury.

KING OF THE countryside's broadleaf trees and a tree deeply ingrained in British culture, the mighty oak is at its magnificent best in the countryside, in woodlands and as single field trees. With great spreading branches, textured grey bark and clothed in leaves which are always a wonderful green but in early spring are an almost fluorescent green, the oak is out on its own. Oaks will live for hundreds of years, and grow to 30 m, but they do not produce acorns until they are at least 40 years old. Oak was used in shipbuilding in former times, when thousands of trees were cut for the building of a single man-of-war. The tree was literally Britain's defence: 'Spread, then, thy sails where naval glory calls, / Britain's best bulwarks are her wooden walls.' ('A Naval Ode' by Henry Green, purser of His Majesty's ship, *Ramillies*, 1773).

THE COUNTRYSIDE PROVIDES many gladdening sights, and near the top of most people's lists would have to be the drifts of bluebells carpeting a woodland floor at this time of year. The particular shade of blue, the plant's form, the effect en masse; this is part of the magic of a countryside spring. In Scotland the common bluebell is known as wild hyacinth. The widely distributed harebell shares some similarities with bluebells but flower much later, in July through September. In Scotland, *this* is their bluebell.

Landscape and Culture

WHEN WALKING IN the countryside there are literally thousands of public footpaths, towpaths and bridleways to be enjoyed. Most are well signposted and take one through the heart of Britain, often on paths that follow routes that date back to the Middle Ages, or further. You are literally walking through time as you take in views that may be little changed from hundreds of years ago.

FINGERPOSTS (OR GUIDE posts) on pathways range from traditional wooden designs to later versions with metal poles and signs in black and white. Such posts are also associated with the canal network. One of the oldest fingerposts in Britain is one which once stood near Chipping Campden, Gloucestershire. It dates to the 1660s and points to Oxford, Gloucester, Warwick and Worcester. Known as Izods Post or Cross Hands, it can be seen in the old police station at Chipping Campden, bearing still its inscription telling the miles: '*NI 1669 Way to... Gloster XVIII, Oxford XXIII, Woster XVI, Warwick XV*'.

THE VARIED FORM of fences, gates and stiles are notable as they reflect locally available materials and architectural styles, for example: the Dorset rod gate, the Herefordshire gate, cleft rail fencing and cleft park railing. In addition to traditional stiles there are ladder stiles, stiles inset into rock walls, and squeeze stiles – gaps in stone walls just wide enough to allow people through, but not animals.

April

AT THE ENTRANCE to old churchyards are gates called lychgates. These are in the form of a roofed porch gateway at the entrance to a churchyard. The meaning of the Old English 'lych' is 'corpse', and it was at the lychgate that pallbearers would wait to meet the clergy and where part of the burial service might be read before the procession went into the graveyard. Some lychgates featured large stone ledges on which the corpse was laid.

A CHARACTERISTIC FEATURE of the countryside, especially in hill country and in the north and west (e.g. Yorkshire and Derbyshire) are drystone walls – known as dykes in Scotland – which are constructed without using mortar. Their durability and stability are testament to the skills of the craftsmen who made them. During the time of the enclosures, many hundreds and even thousands of miles of walls were built by walling gangs which travelled across the countryside. The stone used was, in the main, whatever was at hand from nearby cleared fields. The walls were required to have openings for livestock to move between fields, and often this was achieved by way of the 'sheep-creep'; an opening at the bottom of a wall, filled in above, that was large enough for sheep to use. The filled-in stone layer was often capable of being removed to allow cows to pass through.

Tips

WHEN RAMBLING THROUGH the countryside you can't go wrong in keeping an Ordnance Survey map at hand. OS maps not only show all public paths and bridleways but also show enormous amounts of other information for countryside visitors: local archaeology and history, land use, and natural and built features.

APRIL IS BLUEBELL month, and if you're looking for places to see them, try one of the following selection: Trench Wood, Worcestershire; Winkworth Arboretum, Surrey; Long Wood in Cheddar Gorge, Somerset; Hackfall Wood near Ripon, Yorkshire; Brede High Woods, East Sussex; Heartwood Forest, Hertfordshire; Bovey Valley Woods, Devon; Hole Park Gardens, near Cranbrook, Kent, and Carnmoney Hill, Newtonabbey, County Antrim. But don't be fooled by imposters: there is only one true native English bluebell. It is distinguished from the non-native Spanish bluebell by its beautiful scent (the Spanish bluebell is unscented) and cream anthers at the ends of the stamens (the Spanish bluebells' are blue).

April

WHILE BRITAIN HAS less forest cover than some of its European neighbours, what is does have is ancient trees. So much so that it is said Richmond Park in South London has more 500-year-old trees than Germany and France combined. And a number of those British trees are vastly older than 500 years. Some of our notable ancient trees which you can visit are: the Fortingall Yew, near Aberfeldy, Perthshire (which is possibly as much as 5,000 years old); the Bowthorpe Oak, Bourne, Lincolnshire (over 1,000 years old, and such a huge tree that in the eighteenth century it was rumoured that the hollow inside its trunk was used to accommodate dinner parties); and the Major Oak, Sherwood Forest, Nottinghamshire (Britain's most iconic old tree and considered to be between 800 and 1,000 years old; its branches spread to over 28 m).

Notes

1
....

2
....

3
....

4
....

5
....

6
....

7
....

8
....

9
....

10
....

11
....

12
....

13
....

14
....

April

15

16

17

18

19

20

21

22

23

24

25

26

27

28

29

30

May

LATE SPRING. MILDER days now although at times, as Shakespeare had it, 'Rough winds do shake the darling buds of May'. More than just hawthorn is a-flower; lanes and glades, field margins and byways, stream banks and roadsides are blooming with buttercup, columbine and iris. The young of countryside birds and mammals are beginning to be seen. On farms there's silage being made and, in some parts, first shearings. Wheat and barley stems are lengthening.

Wildlife

WOODPECKERS UTILISE A unique adaptation, in this case the ability to find food under the bark of trees and to drill out nesting holes in tree trunks using their strong beaks. In Britain three kinds are seen; the great spotted, the green, and the lesser spotted. The great spotted is about the size of a blackbird with a graphic black and white appearance, the male showing a red patch at the back of the head. The lesser spotted is the smallest of the three birds. It is also black–white and in the male the whole top of the head is red. The green woodpecker is the largest; green on its upper parts, paler on the belly, with the rump showing bright yellow and a red cap to its head.

THE SIMILARLY FEATURED swift, swallow, and house martin are true aerial acrobats, diving, swooping and wheeling over pastures, ponds and rooftops in their search for a meal. The swift is the largest of the three and leads a remarkable life. Almost its entire life is spent flying. It lands very rarely, mostly when mating – although they can mate on the wing – and when raising its young at the nest. Otherwise, food, water and even sleep are all taken on the wing. Unsurprisingly, the bird's legs are insufficiently developed to support its weight in perching and it is hardly able to walk, should it land on the ground. Summer breeding in Britain, the swift overwinters in Africa, as do swallows and martins. Plumage is an all-over dark brown-black. Birds circling high in the sky will be swifts: swallows work closer to ground level.

SWALLOWS ARE SMALLER and more slender than swifts and are dark glossy-blue on their backs, creamy-yellow on the underside of the body and red on the throat. The tail is much more forked and longer than the swift's. Open pasture and wetlands where insects are plentiful are favourite haunts. In the countryside swallows make their nests in and under the roofs of farm buildings and under bridges and other similar structures to which cup-shaped nests of mud and grass can be adhered.

THE HOUSE MARTIN is the smallest of these birds. Upper-body colouring is more black than the dark blue of the swallow but repeats the swallow's creamy-white underparts while also showing white feathering on the lower back. Bodies and wings are blunter and stubbier. As with swifts and swallows, house martins overwinter in sub-Saharan Africa. House martins often nest in colonies, in holes and scrapes in cliffs and caves.

FINCHES ARE DISTINGUISHED by their strong, rounded bills – strong enough in some species to crack cherry stones – and most are wonderful songsters. Those seen in Britain include a number of summer migrants and winter visitors as well as residents. Most well-known of this group of birds are the goldfinch (red, white and black face, black and gold wings), the chaffinch (pink-orange on breast and cheeks, blue-grey cap) and the greenfinch. Other finches include the crossbill, serin, bullfinch, linnet, siskin, and the wonderfully named brambling and twite. They display typical flocking behaviour when on the move in search of food and in preparation for roosting. A group of goldfinches is known as a 'charm'.

AFTER BECOMING NEARLY extinct in the last century, the otter is today making a comeback in many parts of Britain. Following a ban on hunting and campaigns to reduce the harmful pesticide runoff into river habitats that killed the fish that otter eat, populations are increasing. While not yet widespread, otters are now being seen in places they had not been for more than a hundred years. Otters are night hunters, spending the daytime under cover or inside their holts on riversides.

IF YOU'RE WANTING to see otters, you can experience them at a number of wildlife sites in parts of Britain, among them Cricklepit Mill in Exeter, Devon, Ranworth Broad in Norfolk and Aughton Woods in Lancashire.

Field and Flower

THE MONTH OF May finds its echo in the frothy white flowering of hawthorn – the 'may' of hedgerows. Thorniness and a dense form make hawthorn ideal as a quick-growing stock-proof hedge. An ancient tree of the countryside, its durability is demonstrated by the Hethel Old Thorn, a hawthorn standing in a Norfolk reserve that is estimated at 700 years of age. The hawthorn's flowers develop into deep red fruits known as 'haws', sought after by birds and human wild-food foragers alike – the latter pick them to use in jams and syrups.

THIS MONTH SEES an explosion in small flowering plants of the wayside and hedge margins, among them the aptly named speedwell, comprising a number of creeping plants bearing spikes of mainly blue flowers (some varieties have white and lilac). Most commonly seen is the germander speedwell, whose blue flowers have white centres.

WILD CRABAPPLES LEND a pretty pink and white colouring to hedgerows in the spring. A member of the genus *Malus*, its thorns (which have been bred out of modern forms) are a reminder of its position in the Rosaceae (rose) family of plants. Small greenish-yellow fruits follow the tree's flowers. Wild apple trees also appear in hedgerows and road margins, although it's thought that many are not true native wild apples but rather wilded domestic apple types that have grown from the pips of apple cores tossed out of car windows.

THE COMMON BEECH is a classic and elegant broadleaf tree. Beech woodland is characteristically densely carpeted with the fallen leaves and seed of the trees, whose tannin reduces the number of plants that grow in the tree's understory. Beech is one of the species that are commonly coppiced. The copper beech is a naturally occurring variant of the common beech.

AT ONE TIME a yellow field signified mustard, grown for its seed and as a fodder crop and green manure. Mustard isn't grown as much today – and mostly in Anglia when it is – and the vivid yellow lighting up the landscape this month is now almost sure to be rapeseed. Rapeseed is in great demand for the oil pressed from its seeds and as animal feed.

AS TEMPERATURES START to rise, sheep flocks in the higher parts of the country will be driven up into the hills. One of the hill breeds is the Cheviot – a handsome, sturdy-looking animal with fine white hair on its face, head and legs. The fleece is white, firm and thick with no coloured wool. Cheviots originate and take their name from the Cheviot Hills on the border between Scotland and England. Some rams have horns.

A STURDY MUSCULAR sheep with a distinctive all-black head and legs free of wool, the Suffolk thrives in wet conditions and is not affected by the foot diseases that can trouble other breeds. It was first recognised as a pure breed in 1810, the result of crossing Southdown rams and Norfolk Horned ewes. Suffolks were known originally as Southdown Norfolks or just 'Black Faces'.

Landscape and Culture

MANY COUNTRYSIDE CUSTOMS and traditions have evolved over hundreds and thousands of years, often with their exact origins unknown but regularly attributed to Anglo-Saxon or Celtic tradition, and sometimes from even further back. Some customs, such as maypole dancing, derive from northern European folk festivals that continue in Europe today. In Britain the May Day festival celebrates the arrival of spring and is considered to have arisen from the ancient Germanic reverence for trees and forests, the maypole a representation of the tree as a symbol of fertility. Maypole celebrations more or less disappeared in Britain after the arrival of Christianity but were revived in Victorian times. Today maypole dancing is celebrated in a number of villages on May Day.

WORLD-FAMOUS FOR ITS weather, Britain's climate is influenced by the Atlantic to the west, and the great landmasses of Europe and Africa to the east and south, mixing together Gulf Stream warming, polar blasts from the Arctic, warm air flows from Africa and low-pressure Atlantic systems. Boring it is not, but blessed instead; the countryside's glorious green the result of ample rain. Wrote W. H. Auden of the British landscape: 'If this is the landscape that we, the inconstant ones, are constantly homesick for, it is chiefly because it happens to dissolve in water.'

THE FIRST EVER Dawn Chorus Day – to celebrate songbirds and their chorus of welcome to the new day – was held at Moseley Bog, Birmingham, in 1984. The day, celebrated on the first Sunday in May, is now an international event. At places around Britain on the day you can join in with early morning listening to the joyous song of robins, blackbirds, blackcaps, thrushes, sparrows, larks and more. The first birds get into the act around 4 a.m. but the dawn chorus is probably best heard up to an hour later when the most birds are involved. Recent decades have seen an alarming decline in the number of Britain's songbirds in the countryside due to loss of habitat for nesting places and feeding areas, as well as predation.

FARM HORSES WERE agriculture's tractors in former times, and in some parts of Britain are still used – especially in areas where the ground is boggy and tractors have difficulty, or where there's a danger of machinery adversely compacting the soil. Native British workhorses are powerfully built, some tracing lineage to horses bred in medieval times to carry the weight of a knight in armour. As well as the familiar Clydesdale, the largest of the workhorses, the Suffolk Punch (broad and deep-bodied on short legs) and the Shire (similar to the Clydesdale but taller) are also used.

Tips

MAY IS THE month for elderflowers – you might be familiar with elderflower cordial, elderflower champagne and elderberry jam, but you may not be aware that the flowers are edible in themselves. Try elderflower fritters as an alternative treat. Picking the elderflowers when the flower buds have just opened – before they brown around the edges – is the key for the best flavour. Prepare a thin batter into which the entire flower head should be dipped before deep-frying. Once fried, dip the flower heads into caster sugar then eat. A little cinnamon sprinkled over doesn't go amiss.

NETTLE STINGS CAN be a pain, literally. The needle-like hairs that cover the leaves break off when brushed against by an arm or leg and then penetrate the skin, injecting their irritant, which quickly stings and itches. A tip for some immediate relief is to take a dock leaf – docks will often be found in proximity to nettles and are notable for their large deep-green coloured leaves with slightly reddish stems – and rub it over the affected area. You can also try mashing up a few nettle leaves and spreading the paste over the stinging part. If a natural remedy doesn't work for you, calamine lotion or other antihistamines can help.

THE KIND AND frequency of the drumming sound
woodpeckers make in spring when hammering their
beaks against branches and tree trunks – in order
to state territory or attract a mate – can help you
identify which species it is. The great spotted makes
1–2-second bursts of loud drumming of about 10–30
strikes per second, while the lesser spotted's drumming
is of fewer strikes (less than 10) over a longer time.
The green woodpecker drums only infrequently, more
softly and over a longer duration.

Notes

1
....

2
....

3
....

4
....

5
....

6
....

7
....

8
....

9
....

10
....

11
....

12
....

13
....

14
....

May

15 ....

16 ....

17 ....

18 ....

19 ....

20 ....

21 ....

22 ....

23 ....

24 ....

25 ....

26 ....

27 ....

28 ....

29 ....

30 ....

31 ....

June

EARLY SUMMER. TREES *are in full leaf, the landscape a verdant patchwork of varying greens and yellow. On the air is the buzz of insects and the scent of herbs such as thyme. Banks, hedgerows and fields are alive with butterflies and small birds, and lifted by the colour of bramble in blossom, the pinks and blues of vetches and forget-me-nots, the pink and white of clover and wild roses and the yellow of buttercups in the wetter pastures. If the weather becomes hot and settled there may be a first cut of hay at the end of June.*

Wildlife

UP WITH THE larks! While the skylark's appearance can be described as ordinary – a camouflaging streaky-brown colouring – not so its wonderful towering song. Flying steeply upwards to hang high in the sky over its grassland habitat, 'the lark ascending's stirring song is a quintessential summer sound. The liquid notes just peal out. Two other larks are also seen: the shore lark, a winter visitor from northern Europe, and the woodlark, of a small resident population.

WHEN DEALING WITH the crow family of birds, telling your carrion crow from ravens from rooks can be testing. As a rule of thumb, if there are a lot of crows together then chances are it is a gathering of rooks. If you see a medium-sized black crow-like bird on its own then it is probably a carrion crow. Although carrion crows will flock together when roosting, it is rooks that are the more sociable, nesting together in colonies – rookeries – in the tops of trees (and making a big noise about it), while carrion crows don't. If the crow you're looking at is big and black, then it's most likely a raven. Any small black crows are probably jackdaws. Other members of the crow family seen in Britain include the magpie, jay, and the endangered chough.

THE RAVEN IS glossy black all over. This is a big bird, growing to over 60-cm long and with a wingspan of up to about 1.5 m (about half as big again as the size of a rook or crow's wingspan). Usually seen on its own or as one of a pair, the raven inhabits forests and rocky habitats along coastlines. Its diamond-shaped tail differs from the rounded tail of the carrion crow.

THE CARRION CROW's black plumage has a greenish gloss with a beak that is shorter and less strong-looking than the raven's. The closely related hooded crow is found in Scotland and Ireland, where they have the nickname 'hoodies'. It differs from the carrion crow in having a mix of grey and black plumage on the body with a black head and throat.

SIMILAR IN SIZE to the carrion crow, the rook is distinguished by the greyish white of its face and the bare skin about the base of the beak in the adult bird. The plumage has a purplish sheen to it. The bill is also more pointed than that of the carrion crow.

DRAGONFLIES AND RELATED damselflies can now be seen at the edges of ponds, streams and lakes, skimming the surfaces in their search for the flying insects that make up their diet. Given that dragonflies can fly at up to 37 mph, most of the predated flying insects come off second best. Short-lived in their adult stage – dragonflies may live for just two or three weeks – the evolution from aquatic nymphs to adulthood can, however, take a year or more: unlike the butterfly which evolves from caterpillar to pupa to flying adult, the dragonfly does not have a pupal stage – the nearly mature nymph emerges from the water and sheds its skin to become a fully formed adult.

June

Field and Flower

WITH ITS LEAVES covered in stinging hairs and found frequently in places where one is walking bare-legged, our familiarity with the stinging nettle is sometimes more than we'd like. On the other hand it is its stinging defence that inhibits grazing animals eating it, meaning the nettle can instead provide food and habitat for myriad insects as well as for the larvae of many native butterflies such as the peacock butterfly and the small tortoiseshell. The nutritious young leaves are edible for humans as well, as a leaf vegetable and also dried as a tea. Of course, as this is Britain, there is an annual World Nettle Eating Championship held each year in Dorset, with the winner being the person who has the greatest accumulated length of nettles, after stripping and eating the raw leaves. A smaller variety is the annual nettle, which is also painful to the touch.

THE FOXGLOVE'S PURPLEY-PINK flowered pyramidal spikes, spotted inside the hanging bells, appear from May through to September in open land, hillside, woodland and waste ground, although the foxglove by nature thrives in dappled shade, being a flower of banks and hedgerows. Poisonous though it is (and potentially deadly poisonous to humans) the foxglove is the original source of digoxin; a medicine used for treating heart conditions. Occasionally pure white wild foxgloves are found.

THE YELLOW IRIS (commonly called 'flag iris') is one of two irises native to Britain, and the most common. It is seen bordering streams and ponds and in damp shaded areas of woodland and in damp meadow, and flowers from May through to June. The other species is the stinking iris – 'stinking' due to the 'offish' smell of the leaves when they are crushed. Flowers are purple-tinged yellow and in autumn its seed pods open to disclose large bright orange seeds.

SEVERAL DOZEN SPECIES of the wild parsley family abound in the countryside, on path sides and road verges and field margins, their flower heads taking the form of clouds of usually white flowers above ferny leaves. Superficially similar, the members include species such as hogweed, wild angelica, cowbane (poisonous), hemlock (also poisonous) and Queen Anne's lace (also known as wild carrot).

ALSO KNOWN AS the linden tree, the lime is a large deciduous broadleaf native tree with bright green leaves, paler on the underside. Its name can be confusing, but there is no connection to the citrus lime. 'Lime' in this case is a corruption of the Middle English and Germanic *lind* (hence the tree's other name), meaning 'light' or 'yielding'. The yellow-green sweet-scented flowers are very attractive to honeybees.

SOME HUNDRED OR more species of wild rose are found in Britain. Common about the countryside on roadside banks and in hedgerows are the arching pink or white-flowered dog-rose; deep pink flowered sweet briar (with leaves that are apple-scented when crushed); white-flowered Burnet; and the field rose with creamy white flowers. All produce colourful hips in autumn.

THE DOG-ROSE WAS the stylised rose of medieval European heraldry, and is the county flower of Hampshire.

Landscape and Culture

Is there a prettier place in the world to be than the country lane? Created for the passage of cattle and sheep to and from pastures or to milking, and great for ambling along under overhanging trees and beside vibrant banks of wildflowers, fields and hedgerows, country lanes lift the heart. They are an encapsulation of the countryside: wildflowers from anemones to yarrow, trees young and old, views across fields of wheat, barley and oats and pasture grazed by sheep and cattle. There are sounds such as the cawing of crows in treetops and the chatter of flocking finches. The movement from flitting butterflies and swooping swallows, the occasional rustle in the undergrowth that might be mice or a rabbit, the smell of earth and grass… heaven is a country lane in spring.

A big part of its charm and an important part of the history of the rural landscape is the hedgerow. (Britain's hedgerows are old, with around a third of hedge trees estimated at over a century old.) And not only do they add beauty to the landscape but they are also vital for wildlife. The traditional mixed hedgerow includes a variety of trees such as the mainstay hawthorn, blackthorn, hazel, oak and field maple, grown for their wood, as well as other trees grown for their fruits to provide forage food in the autumn. Herbs, grasses and climbing plants soon established themselves and after a number of years the hedgerow was providing protection, food and shelter for a wide variety of birds and small mammals and invertebrates.

A FEATURE OF Scotland's western coastal Highlands and western islands are the crofts that dot the landscape. These farmhouses are part of the crofting system of farming that has existed in Scotland for hundreds of years as a means of subsistence farming tenure. Tenants pay a small rent for their croft and share grazing communally. Typically the crofts have a small amount of flat land for individual growing of crops in addition to the communal grazing for sheep and cattle on hill land.

Tips

THIS IS OF course the season of festivals and fairs across the country, and it is easy enough to plan your summer itinerary to take in one or more of these. They range from old-fashioned village fairs – think flower- and best vegetable-growing competitions and home baking – through to big events such as regional agricultural shows, game fairs, food festivals and highland games that run over a number of days and which are visited by thousands of people. Music festivals also seem to take place somewhere in the countryside almost every weekend between now and September.

BICYCLES WERE MADE for touring the countryside. Like walking, bikes are a quiet means of transport, but with the added benefit that you can cover a great deal more ground than walking when you want to. From idling along canal towpaths to exploring woodland trails and country lanes, the countryside offers a host of opportunities – and mostly on gentle gradients! Local bike hires abound, as do enjoyable touring routes, a selection of which are provided here. Details for each can be found through local tourist information sites. It goes without saying that most of them pass pubs.

Norfolk: From King's Lynn to Snettisham. From the historic medieval port of King's Lynn into the countryside of West Norfolk – woodland, wading birds and more. 16 miles.

Hampshire: From Fordingbridge to Brockenhurst. Circular rides up to about 20 miles in length can be made through the beautiful New Forest – great views, glades and shallow rivers. Gravel tracks.

Shropshire: From Gobowen to Colemere – into North Shropshire's land of fens and canals and via the pretty market town of Ellesmere. 14 miles.

Essex: From Colchester to Hadleigh – through the beautiful 'Constable Country'. 15 miles.

Hertfordshire: From Aldbury to Frithsden – scenic Hertfordshire. 15 miles.

West Yorkshire: From Hebden Bridge to Todmorden – via the Rochdale Canal. 9 miles.

Northumberland: From North Sunderland to Bamburgh – coastal route to the castle at Bamburgh. 15 miles.

WHEN YOU'RE THINKING about accommodation in the countryside, one unique option is a farm stay on a working farm. Lots of these are available around Britain and put you into the heart of farming.

Notes

1
....

2
....

3
....

4
....

5
....

6
....

7
....

8
....

9
....

10
....

11
....

12
....

13
....

14
....

June

15
....

16
....

17
....

18
....

19
....

20
....

21
....

22
....

23
....

24
....

25
....

26
....

27
....

28
....

29
....

30
....

July

MIDSUMMER. THE START of the dog days. It's balmy now with perhaps some summer thunderstorms at times. Grasslands and meadows show sweeps of colour with daisies, native orchids and poppies. At ponds and streams dragonflies skim the water while kingfishers and grey herons wait their chance. Fewer new flowers now on fruiting shrubs and plants and trees – instead energy is spent on swelling fruit and setting seed ahead of nature's autumn deadline. In the fields, ewes and their grown-up lambs seek shade under oaks and hedgerows.

Wildlife

THE DIPPER – a rounded, short-tailed, rather wren-like bird – occupies a unique niche in bird life. Exclusively confined to the edge of streams where it feeds on aquatic insects and small fish, the dipper can be seen perching on rocks in the water and dipping down into the water to catch its prey. It will also dive down into the water, swimming after its food and even walking underwater on stream beds in pursuit.

THE ADDER (OR viper) is the most common of the three snakes native to Britain, and the only poisonous one. The others are the smooth snake and the grass snake. Adders are readily identified by the dark zigzag markings along their backs which are usually of a pale yellow, brown or silvery colour. They may be found in dry countryside such as heathland and rough ground; the adder will often be lying out in the sun, perhaps on a stony path in order to maximise the heat. Its diet comprises small mammals such as mice and lizards. While its poison is capable of killing a human, fatalities are rare. The poison is said to be more potent in March and April when they first emerge from hibernation. The adder is about 45–60 cm long and its eyes have slit-shaped pupils, rather than the round pupils of the other species.

THE SMOOTH SNAKE is rare and totally harmless. Distribution is restricted to heathland in southern England. As its name suggests, the smooth snake is notable for the absence of ridges on its scales, which the two other species do possess. Dull brown or dark grey in colouring, a dark strip runs across the eye. Like the grass snake, the pupils of its eyes are round (not the slit pupils of the adder). They are usually about 70-cm long.

GRASS SNAKES, ALSO completely harmless, are more common than adders. Preferring damper conditions than adders, grass snakes live in woodland and meadows. Its upper side is olive-brown, the sides of the body marked by vertical black barrings, and the snake's collar is black and light yellow. It has round pupils, the same as the smooth snake, and is about 1.2-m long.

THERE ARE AROUND 60 native butterfly species resident in Britain, along with about 2,500 species of moth. Summer migrants from Europe add to the total. Butterfly groups include brown butterflies, fritillaries, whites, skippers, coppers, hairstreaks, tortoiseshells, peacocks and ringlets. The species most commonly seen in the countryside include the small white, red admiral, painted lady, peacock, meadow brown and small tortoiseshell. Worryingly, three-quarters of native species are in decline as a result of massive habitat loss and degradation: populations have reduced by as much as half since 1990.

Field and Flower

As WELL AS grazing the usual farming grasslands, beef cattle are also often used to graze some of Britain's natural grasslands in order to maintain their ecosystems for native wildlife. Such conservation grazing controls scrub and encourages the growth of wildlife-friendly flowers and grasses which then become habitats attractive to insects, butterflies and ground-nesting birds. Human activity shaped Britain's moorland, meadows, heaths and grasslands, and regular grazing is a way to maintain the habitats that were so formed. The dung from cattle is important as well; the cowpats finding favour with numerous insect species that go on to be food for birds, bats and other animals.

ONE OF BRITAIN'S oldest beef cattle breeds is the Galloway, which is descended from two ancient Scottish breeds. Galloway are noted for their thick, woolly hides. Another notable beef breed is the Hereford, first bred in Herefordshire around 300 years ago – at the time of the Industrial Revolution when expanding urban populations increased the demand for meat.

THE HORSE CHESTNUT was introduced to Britain in around 1600. It is a simply beautiful tree whether singly in a field, or in small groups. The candle-like white blossoms that appear in May draw the eye. Now the tree's seeds – called conkers and used in the famous game – are ripening within spiky husks. Confusion arises with the sweet chestnut (or Spanish chestnut) that produces nuts of a similar appearance, but which are edible (horse chestnuts are inedible and even mildly poisonous to humans).

ONCE A COMMON flower of grain fields, the vibrant red poppy is one of many field flowers that has suffered at the hands of modern farming practices in the use of herbicides and improved screening of seeds. Britain's fields were once altogether more colourful, with, in addition to the red of poppies, corn buttercups, vetches and the Venus' looking glass. Intensification has little room for what are seen as weeds. Given the red poppy's association with Remembrance Day, it's more than a little ironic that soon wild poppies will have slipped from memory.

DAISIES ARE FOUND across Britain on grasslands from the coast to the uplands. The ox-eye daisy is the common wild daisy – white petals around a yellow centre. A flower that for many people symbolises traditional grassland meadows, the ox-eye daisy also thrives on banks and cliffs. Its early name of 'day's eye' stemmed from its habit of closing up its petals on dull days and at night-time, which, over time, became contracted to 'daisy'.

Landscape and Culture

GRAIN CROPS SUCH as wheat, rye, barley and oats are known in Britain collectively as 'corn', not to be confused with the American 'corn' or sweet corn (traditionally called 'maize' by Britons). The Old English word 'corn' derives from the Old Frisian 'korn', which is still the German word for 'grain'.

CORN DOLLIES ARE symbols of good luck, which are plaited from stems of grain, and have their origin in old European harvest customs for ensuring a good harvest the next season. The belief was that a spirit inhabited the corn crops and that harvesting the grain destroyed the spirit's home. Cutting the last sheaf of a harvest was considered unlucky so instead, to appease the corn spirit, the last standing stems would be plaited into a 'dolly' as a home for the spirit. The dolly would be ceremoniously taken back to the village for keeping over winter and then ploughed back into the soil of the next season's crop.

July

WILDFLOWER MEADOWS ARE a habitat essential to much of Britain's wildlife. For insects, who are attracted to the flowers for their food and which then pollinate them; for bird species that feed on the insects; for other ground-nesting species that utilise the shelter and hiding places the grasses provide; and for rare flowers such as orchids that can survive at the damp base of such fields.

BUT THE MEADOW is a disappearing habitat. It is estimated that more than 90 per cent of the old flower-rich meadows that existed in 1950 have gone. Many people these days may never have seen one. It's not just the physical loss but the cultural and psychological loss as well. Meadows are part of our evolution, the names of its animals and flowers embedded in our language. They are paradisiacal places of sweet grass, colourful wildflowers, butterflies and birds, the click of grasshoppers and the sky stretching above, and we allow them to go at great risk to ourselves and to the countryside.

Tips

WHEN OUT WALKING you may notice in some fields that a margin border around the crop or ploughed field has been left for wild grasses and wildflowers to grow long and high. This is likely to be part of a fairly new initiative by British farmers to create more habitat areas for wildlife such as the endangered harvest mouse. The flowers and grasses provide a welcome food source for butterflies, whose numbers have declined greatly in recent years because there are fewer wildflowers in fields. The changes in farming practices and in the rural landscape over the last 40 years – including the increased use of herbicides and pesticides, the amalgamation of fields and the loss of hedgerows – have all contributed to massive falls in the populations of most countryside-dwelling animal species.

THIS MONTH AND next are summer's hottest – the 'dog days of summer'. The term originated with the Romans, who believed that the closeness of the Dog Star, Sirius, to the earth at this time engendered particularly hot weather. The period runs for 40 days from 3 July to 11 August. Be warned, then, of sweltering weather during which, it was thought, the 'Sea boiled, the Wine turned sour, Dogs grew mad, and all other creatures became languid,' according to John Brady in his 1813 treatise on the calendar *Clavis Calendaria*.

July

JULY IS A good month to take in the romance of traditional flower meadows. There are a number of organisations working to protect these traditional habitats, active in their conservation for reasons of their beauty, biodiversity and as habitats and food sources for wildlife. There are many easily accessible flower meadows to visit in Britain including: Rose End Meadows near Cromford, Derbyshire (cowslips, and buttercups and cow parsley in spring); Marden Meadow near Cranbrook, Kent (hay meadow, comprising numerous wildflowers along with vetches and wild grasses); Kingcombe Meadows in Lower Kingcombe, Dorset (traditionally managed and home to old-time wildflowers such as lady's mantle and Devil's-bit scabious); Foster's Green Meadows in Bromsgrove, Worcestershire (never treated with chemicals and today home to nearly 200 plants including green-winged orchids and meadow saffron in autumn); The Knapp and Papermill Nature Reserve in Bridges Stone, Worcestershire (walking to the reserve takes you through hay meadows and old orchards, and the reserve's flowers attract dozens of species of butterfly); Aldbury Nowers in Tring, Hertfordshire (another fine butterfly habitat); and Chyverton Nature Reserve near Truro in Cornwall (flower-rich meadows and old hedgerows).

Notes

1
....

2
....

3
....

4
....

5
....

6
....

7
....

8
....

9
....

10
....

11
....

12
....

13
....

14
....

July

15
....

16
....

17
....

18
....

19
....

20
....

21
....

22
....

23
....

24
....

25
....

26
....

27
....

28
....

29
....

30
....

31
....

August

LATE SUMMER. THE month of abundance as fruits and seeds of wild vines and trees start to ripen. August's flowers include harebell, meadow cranesbill, meadowsweet, goldenrod and betony. Sparrows and finches are on the wing and thrushes and blackbirds are feeding on rowan berries. Hay fields are being cut and grain brought into storage. Finches will flock to feed on the stubble in the fields before it is turned into the soil and preparations begin for next year's crops.

Wildlife

EIGHTEEN SPECIES OF bat are found in Britain, the most numerous of which are the common and soprano pipistrelle bats. These are smallish in the bat scheme of things, with wingspans of only about 220 mm. At the other end of the scale is the greater horseshoe with a wingspan of up to 400 mm. The various species roost in tunnels, lofts, under bridges, in caves and in old buildings, including belfrys. Some of these colonies may number as many as a thousand individuals. They hibernate over winter.

MOST COMMON OF the five species of owl that breed in the countryside is the tawny (or brown) owl, also sometimes called the screech owl, at 38 cm in height. The slightly smaller barn owl is less common but more widespread across Britain. Both hunt small mammals such as mice and voles, usually swallowing prey whole with the indigestible parts such as bones and fur later regurgitated in pellet form. Barn owls don't build nests and instead lay their eggs on flat surfaces, inside a building if possible. The tawny owl does nest-build, preferring holes in trees. Daytime is spent roosting (although the little owl can be seen in the daylight perching high), with owls on the wing to hunt at dusk and dawn in the main. With a noiseless wingbeat and light-sensitive eyes that enable them to see in blackness, owls are brilliantly adapted for stalking flight at nights.

BRITAIN IS HOME to three native lizards – the common lizard, the sand lizard and the slow worm, which despite its snake-like appearance is in fact a legless lizard. The common lizard is the most widespread, found across Britain in a wide range of habitats. It is about 15 cm long including its tail and is a greyish-brown with darker markings on its back. The sand lizard is restricted to a handful of counties and in these prefers dunes, heaths and dry woodlands; it is similarly coloured to the common lizard but a little larger. The slow worm is larger again, growing up to 46 cm long, its colouring bronze with a stripe along the middle of its back. It is found in damp areas of woodland margins. All three lizards are able to shed their tails if attacked as a diversion to allow them to escape. Non-native species include the common wall lizard and the western green lizard.

Field and Flower

THE ENGLISH ELM is another of the classic broadleaf trees of the countryside, towering to 36 m. These are the trees of Constable's and Turner's paintings, the great trees that landowners and farmers planted not just for their timber but also for their beauty and once numbered in their millions across Britain. But sadly no longer, since Dutch elm disease in the 1970s reduced the population so dramatically that today there are only perhaps a few thousand left in the countryside. Brighton is home to the National Elm Collection, which includes the 'Preston Twins', considered to be the oldest surviving English elms in Europe. The trees are home to the elm-dependent white-letter hairstreak butterfly, a species which lives mainly at treetop level on the elm.

THE TEASEL IS a grassland and stream-bank plant with prickly stems and compact spiky flower heads bearing pinky-purple flowers. It is perhaps best known for the conical seed heads that follow, flowering in July and August. One variety of teasel was once much used in the woollen industry, the hooked seed heads used to lift the nap on newly woven cloth. While they have mainly been replaced today by metal cards to do this job, some weavers still prefer to use teasel heads, claiming it gives a better result. Teasel seed heads are also an important source of winter food for birds such as finches.

THE CREAMY PINK flowers of the twining wild honeysuckle, also known as woodbine, are sweetly scented – a scent that increases in the evening in order to attract the moths that pollinate it. Honeysuckle is a bank and hedgerow plant, preferring damp coolness at its roots and a position from which it can climb into sunlight.

MEADOWSWEET IS A robust, attractive herb with fragrant white flowers, and is found in ditches and water meadows. The plant contains natural salicylic acid which is used for pain relief, and this connection gave aspirin its name – the 'spir' of 'aspirin' from the plant's former genus name, *Spiraea*.

BRITAIN IS HOME to dozens of varieties of wild orchids, including the common spotted orchid, lady's slipper, the purply-brown flowered bee orchid, and the green-flowered twayblade. Ranging in height from just a few centimetres to 1.2 m and more, orchids are found in woodlands, grasslands and marshes. Many wild orchids are rare and all are protected – it is illegal to pick them or dig them up. So rare is the ghost orchid that no sightings of it were made for 23 years until a single bloom was discovered in 2010.

Landscape and Culture

THERE ARE SOMETHING like 16,000 parish churches in Britain spanning nearly a thousand years of architectural styles, beginning with Norman architecture following the Conquest. Those churches in villages across the countryside have been at the heart of local farming communities for hundreds of years, and for many of the villages the church may be its oldest surviving building. Churches were once the centres of their communities, not just in religious life but also as a meeting place for local guilds, as courtrooms, repositories of wills and of course as the place that held the registers of births and baptisms, marriages and deaths.

CASTLES CAME TO Britain with the Normans in 1066 – originally as fortified structures that were raised by feudal barons and members of the monarchy. Hundreds of such defensive fortifications were built around Britain, many of which remain today. The structure evolved from a simple defensible tower set on a 'motte' – a raised steep-sided flat-topped area of ground – around which a ditch was dug. For defence the ditch was lined with sharp stakes or filled with water. Over time 'motte' came to refer to a water-filled ditch around the raised ground, hence 'moat' today. In the following centuries castles developed to include high stone walls, stone towers and keeps, portcullises and drawbridges.

THE WORD 'BARN' is derived from the Old English 'bere' for barley – a 'bern' was a house in which barley was stored. Barley was the main crop grown by Anglo-Saxon farmers. Traditional stone barns from later periods can still be seen in the countryside, some dating from medieval times.

BRITISH PLACE NAMES reflect their derivation from old Celtic, Anglo-Saxon, Scandinavian and Norman names. Viking and Norman invaders left their mark; 'fell', as used in the north of England and the south of Scotland for 'mountain', comes from Old Norse – e.g. Scafell in the Lake District and Culter Fell in Lanarkshire. Following the withdrawal of Roman legions from Britain, Anglo-Saxons began settling here from about the fifth century. Their settlements are identifiable by the hundreds of place names ending in 'ing' (such as Hastings), 'ham' (Birmingham) and 'ton' (Luton) across Britain, among others. As with place names, field names can also tell us much about the landscape, often being a pointer to what their ancient usage may have been – such as 'iron acre', which could suggest iron mining or manufacture, and 'breck' ('break') for a place of cultivated soil.

Tips

DIP INTO LOCAL history by taking time to visit old churchyards during your travels. Often very quiet, restful places of mossed and titled headstones and undulating ground (probably indicating unmarked graves) they are full of atmosphere. While stone headstones date back only as far as about the seventeenth century, wooden crosses were the norm before that time and these have long-since rotted, so often the churchyards themselves can be considerably older than the stones would lead you to believe. This is evidenced in the ancient church crosses in some graveyards that go back to the beginning of Christianity in Britain, around the fourth century AD. These large stone crosses would be set up to mark places of Christian worship – at times on places where pre-Christian worship had taken place. In following years, the first churches were built around the location of some of these stone crosses.

IF OWLS ARE your thing, there are numerous special places you can go where these magnificent birds are frequently sighted. Note that barn owls are most likely seen in the early dawn and early dusk, flying over rough fields in their hunt for voles and mice. Tawny owls – the ones which make the classic hoot sound – are heard mostly after dusk. Little owls only fly at night; in the daytime in winter you might see one perched in a tree enjoying the sun. Short-eared owls are winter migrants to Britain from northern Europe and may be seen flying in the daytime in winter. Look for owls at the following places:

In the South West:
Windmill Hill, Avebury, Wiltshire
Holnicote Estate, Exmoor, Somerset
South Milton Sands, South Devon

In London and the South East:
Osterley Park, Greater London
Hatchlands Park, Surrey
Polesden Lacey, Surrey
Sissinghurst Castle, Kent

In the Midlands:
Charlecote Park, Warwickshire
Brockhampton Estate, Herefordshire
Calke Abbey, Derbyshire

In Northern Ireland:
Castle Ward, County Down
Murlough National Nature Reserve, County Down
Strangford Lough, County Down
Crom Estate, County Fermanagh

In the East of England:
Orford Ness National Nature Reserve, Suffolk
Wicken Fen, Cambridgeshire
Blickling Estate, Norfolk
Felbrigg Estate, Norfolk

In Wales:
Stackpole Estate, Pembrokeshire
Penbryn Beach, Ceredigion
Llanerchaeron, Ceredigion
Craflwyn, Gwynedd

In the North West:
Quarry Bank Mill, Cheshire
The Atlantic Oakwoods of Borrowdale, Cumbria
Sandscale Haws, Cumbria
Sizergh Castle and Garden, Cumbria
Silverdale, Cumbria

In the North East:
Gibside, Tyne and Wear
Allen Banks and Staward Gorge, Northumberland

Notes

1
....

2
....

3
....

4
....

5
....

6
....

7
....

8
....

9
....

10
....

11
....

12
....

13
....

14
....

August

15

16

17

18

19

20

21

22

23

24

25

26

27

28

29

30

31

September

EARLY AUTUMN. SHORTENING days. Mists and mellow fruitfulness, yes, and mushrooming and changing leaf colour as well. The growing season draws to a close. This month migratory birds will begin to gather for their return to wintering grounds, while animals that hibernate will start feeding up on autumn seeds and fruits ahead of their long winter sleep. On farms, harvest is nearing its end.

Wildlife

THE COUNTRYSIDE IS home to more than a dozen mouse-like mammals including rats, shrews and voles, as well as a number of different kinds of mouse. They range in size from the tiny delicate pygmy shrew at just 4-cm excluding its tail (Britain's smallest rodent) to the 25-cm-long brown rat. They are distinguished from the common grey house mouse by having reddish brown on their upper parts and white-cream underneath. (Despite the name, the dormouse is not in fact a mouse but from a different family of rodents.)

THE LONG TAIL of the delicate harvest mouse is used as a twining support as the animal makes its way through long grass and grain. Its breeding nest is a compact ball of dried grass and leaves set about a metre above the ground and interwoven among plant and shrub stems, or in standing grain. Often thistle down is used to line its nests. The harvest mouse doesn't hibernate but spends wintertime in a burrow underground.

THE MOST COMMONLY seen of the countryside mice is the wood mouse, also known as the long-tailed field mouse. Found in fields, open grassland, scrub and hedgerows where homes are an underground system of burrows, it does not hibernate. The yellow-necked mouse was for many years considered to be the same species as the wood mouse but was eventually given separate status: slightly larger, it has a distinctive yellow neckband and darker colouring.

WHILE RATS, VOLES and mice are gnawing rodents, the shrews are

insectivorous as well as preying on worms. They
are easily distinguished from its mouse cousins by
a much longer nose. There are five shrew species of
which the most widespread is the smallest, the pygmy
shrew. Shrews live in the ground-cover of woods and
grasslands where they make their narrow tunnels. In
order to survive, shrews must eat 2–3 times their body
weight in food each day, which, one imagines, explains
their restless twitchiness and renowned irritability.
They don't hibernate for the same reason.

THE COMMON SHREW is the most frequently seen of the
shrew family. With dark brown velvet-like fur on its upper
parts and silver-grey on its underside and teeth that are
red-tipped due to the iron contained in their enamel. The
iron adds resistance to the enamel, which would otherwise
be worn down with all that eating. The water shrew preys
on crustaceans, fish and frogs in slow-moving streams.

THREE SPECIES OF vole live in Britain; the field vole,
the water vole and the bank vole. All three are widely
distributed across Britain, although the water vole is very
rare. All are herbivores with grass as their main food
source. They can be distinguished from mice by their
rounder faces and shorter ears that are covered with fur.

THE FIELD VOLE is common in grassland and
moorlands where it is a prolific breeder – having as
many as six litters per year and up to seven young each
time. The bank vole is the smallest of the three voles
and lives in hedgerows and woodlands. Largest is the
water vole, at about 18 cm long. Also known as the
water rat (think Ratty from *The Wind in the Willows*)
it makes its home in a network of burrows dug into
the banks of ponds, ditches, rivers and streams close
to their food source of aquatic plants and grasses. The
burrows have entrances underwater as well.

Field and Flower

HORNBEAM TREES CAN be confused with beech given their similar smooth grey bark and oval leaves. The hornbeam's leaves are differentiated by being smaller and more furrowed. Like the beech, the hornbeam also holds onto its dead leaves rather than dropping them, meaning that hornbeam hedges provide year-long protected habitats for roosting and nesting birds, as well as small mammals. Its name derives from Old English 'horn' meaning 'hard', and 'beam' meaning 'tree'. Hornbeam grows wild only in southern parts of Britain.

ELEVEN WILD THISTLE species with their characteristic purple tufted flower heads and prickly leaves – and sometimes stems as well – make their points known across the countryside, particularly at this time of year as they are in flower. One of them – there is debate as to whether it is the cotton thistle or the spear thistle – has been the emblem of Scotland since the thirteenth century.

YARROW FLOWERS FROM June through to September; a common plant of the wayside and in pastures and meadows. Growing to around a metre high with a spreading form, its leaves are almost feathery, the flat-topped clusters of flowers white to pink. Their strong, sweet scent is similar to chrysanthemums. In times gone by, yarrow was included in pasture grasses, partly because its deep roots drew up minerals into the leaves which helped prevent mineral deficiencies in the grazing stock.

SCRAMBLING OVER HEDGEROWS and trees, Britain's only native clematis (called old man's beard or traveller's joy) flowers during August and

September. The seeds that develop retain part of the flowers in the form of grey tufted balls of long feathery hairs – indeed very much like an 'old man's beard'. It was described by sixteenth-century herbalist John Gerard as 'decking and adorning waies and hedges where people trauell'.

DAMP AUTUMN CONDITIONS see the emergence of mushrooms and toadstools this month. Britain is home to thousands of different fungi that can be found in woodlands and fields. Many are poisonous and if wanting to go mushrooming you must ensure you are confident you have correctly identified the species, especially as regards the death cap mushroom. The death cap is responsible for the great majority of human deaths from fungus poisoning. Just an ounce of the death cap is enough to kill you, and there is no known antidote. When it comes to mushrooms and toadstools, the part we see above ground is the plant's fruit; the main part of a fungus is underground in the form of masses of tiny threads running through the surrounding soil.

BEST KNOWN OF the native ferns is bracken, occurring mainly in northern Britain and characteristic of Scotland's upland moorlands. Because of its rapid colonising ability however, it can be a major problem in woodlands, grasslands and old farmland, and on moorlands. It will take over from heather where heather has been overly grazed or burnt, allowing bracken to establish itself on the bare ground that is exposed. Once established, bracken's shading effect and slow-decomposing litter left when it dies off for the winter prevents other plants from growing. Bracken contains a number of toxins and grazing stock cannot be allowed to eat it, so where bracken has invaded farmland this impacts on availability of grazing.

Landscape and Culture

SEPTEMBER BRINGS AUTUMN colours to countryside trees. The coming weeks bring a wonderful opportunity to take in landscapes turning from green through yellows, oranges, reds and purples, and to enjoy the refreshing coolness that has crept into the air. If the summer has been especially warm, this will have increased the trees' sugar content which can mean a great intensity of leaf colour. The National Arboretum at Westonbirt in Gloucestershire includes a number of national collections of trees and at this time of year the Japanese maples especially light up in shades of orange and red.

HARVEST TIME HAS special relevance in the countryside, where there is a deep connection to nature and the harvest bounty is more visible. Festivals celebrating and giving thanks for a successful season go back to ancient times. Harvest festivals today usually take place in September and traditionally as close as possible to the date of the harvest moon, the full moon closest to the autumn equinox. In the past, harvest festivals were held at the beginning of the harvest on 1 August when loaves of bread would be made from the new wheat crop. These loaves would be given to the church and were then used as bread for communion. Later on at harvest's end when all the sheaves were in, there would be a harvest supper for the field workers, usually on Michaelmas Day. Today's church harvest celebrations date back to 1843 when a minister in Cornwall first invited parishioners to celebrate thanksgiving with him in the church.

September

BEFORE THE ADVENT of mechanised harvesters, grain stems were cut and gathered into bunches called sheaves that were stacked in fields in stooks to dry and await carting from the fields for threshing. Modern combine harvesters strip the stems directly and most of the straw is chopped by the machine and spread onto the ground where it will be later turned into the soil. Today any stooks you see are likely to be old-fashioned grain varieties grown for thatching.

AUTUMN'S BERRIES, FRUITS and nuts are a forager's delight. Hedgerows, lanes and field edges promise a cornucopia of berries, sloes, nuts, hips and haws. Make sure you can identify accurately what you're picking, and always wash your harvest well – it's best to avoid picking anything growing in waste ground around old industrial sites where soil might have been contaminated or close to busy roads. Only take just what you need and leave some for others – particularly the wildlife which depend on it for their food.

Tips

Autumn leaf viewing – in addition to the National Arboretum in Westonbirt there are a number of other lovely places throughout Britain where you can be moved by autumn's splendour, such as: Castell Coch in Wales (copper beeches in particular); Batsford Arboretum in the Cotswolds (especially lovely are the cherries and maples); Burnham Beeches in Buckinghamshire (a nature reserve that includes an ancient woodland remnant); Belsay Hall in Northumberland; Grizedale Forest in the Lake District (oaks, larches and elders provide shows of yellow through rust colourings); Sherwood Forest in Nottinghamshire; Lanhydrock in Cornwall (ancient oaks in more than 900 acres of parkland); Stourhead in Wiltshire (maples, beeches and oaks have been planted here to give a wash of autumn colour over the weeks).

When you're out foraging, don't forget rosehips. The orangey-red hips of the dog-rose found in hedgerows are chock-full of vitamin C and can be used to make jams, jellies and syrups and are also good for a tonic drink – a rosehip tea that is good against a cold. (Remove the hairs on the rosehips before using them as these can cause irritation.) Thirty berries are said to contain as much vitamin C as 40 oranges.

IT CAN BE easy to confuse newts seen on land with common lizards as they share a similar colour and size. A few points of differentiation will help you identify which is which: for a start, newts have smooth skin although it sometimes has a warty texture, while lizards' skin is scaly. When disturbed, lizards tend to dart away quickly while newts move more slowly. Finally, if you're close enough to count them, lizards have five toes on their front legs; newts four. If you are lucky enough to spot a great crested newt you'd be wise to leave it in peace as it is illegal to handle or disturb these amphibians without a licence in Britain.

NOISY AND GREGARIOUS, the starling is commonplace enough in towns but in the countryside flocks in huge numbers throughout the year. In the autumn and winter months, before roosting at night, starlings can be seen grouping in their hundreds of thousands, flocking in formations called murmurations that condense and expand, wheel and swoop in unison. 'Murmuration' originally referred to the sound made by the rippling of the starlings' wings, but is now more commonly used to describe this fascinating aerial display in which the murmuration is able to change shape and direction incredibly quickly. It appears each starling follows directions based on the actions of the six or seven birds closest to them. Researchers believe the reasons behind such displays include the sharing of information on feeding places and a way of generating warmth, in addition to its deterrent factor when it comes to birds of prey – safety in numbers.

Notes

1
....

2
....

3
....

4
....

5
....

6
....

7
....

8
....

9
....

10
....

11
....

12
....

13
....

14
....

15

16

17

18

19

20

21

22

23

24

25

26

27

28

29

30

October

Mid-autumn. The days are starting to draw in. Many of the summer-breeding migrant birds such as swifts have departed while the first of the winter visitors are beginning to arrive. Hedgerows are laden with berries. Oaks and hazel trees are searched by squirrels and mice for nuts. In the fields starlings and sparrows join yellowhammers to feed in the stubble. Dairy cows will be brought indoors to spend the winter, feeding on the silage made in the spring.

Wildlife

SIX SPECIES OF deer live wild in Britain – the red deer, roe, fallow, sika, muntjac and Chinese water deer. (*Seven* species in fact if you count a small herd of reindeer in Scotland. Reindeer disappeared from Scotland hundreds of years ago but were re-established in the 1950s by a Swedish reindeer herder.) Deer most likely to be seen are the red, roe and fallow.

THE RED DEER is Britain's largest deer at about 1.2 m and is most numerous in Scotland on open hill land. In other locations it prefers woodlands adjoining open land. At 70 cm high, the roe deer is half the size of its cousin. The fawns are spotted to blend with the dappled background of their woodland habitat.

ORIGINAL FALLOW DEER populations died out in Britain during the last ice age. The species is thought to have been re-introduced twice to Britain since, by the Romans and certainly by the Normans for food. More variable in its colouring than other deer species, there is a white form as well as the familiar dapple–spotted animal. All fawns are spotted at birth. Its preferred habitats are broad-leaved woodlands and open fields.

October

AT THE TOP of Britain's avifauna sits its birds of prey, a group of families – hawks, eagles, falcons and osprey – whose members include some notable individuals. Among them is the buzzard, Britain's most common and widely distributed bird of prey which is seen soaring in slow, wide circles over woodland and moors in its search for small mammals and birds. In the breeding season buzzards perform amazing aerial displays involving upward circling followed by a tumbling fall towards the ground. Its body is about 50 cm long, with dark brown plumage and barring on its tail.

FEWER THAN 500 pairs of golden eagles breed in Britain, where it is confined almost entirely to Scotland. Here you may be fortunate enough to see these magnificent birds soaring, looping and plunging over the wild, open moorlands and mountains of the Scottish Highlands and islands. They can grow up to 102 cm long, with a wingspan of up to 2.3 m, and have golden colouring across their head and breast.

Field and Flower

THE FIELD MAPLE is Britain's only native maple; a picturesque tree usually found in woodlands but also in hedgerows where it's valued for its quick growth. It's one of the native hardwoods used for coppicing. The dark green leaves produce a honeydew attractive to some butterflies. Leaves turn a rich golden yellow in autumn. As with all maple trees, sap from the field maple can be used to make maple syrup.

DURING WINTER, MOST beef cattle are housed in large open barns bedded with straw, usually barley as this is less dusty and brittle than wheat, and is also edible and nutritious for the cattle which will tend to eat some of the new straw when it's laid. Come spring, all of the used straw will be stored and, when it's rotted down, spread as manure over arable fields.

A SMALL EVERGREEN tree, the common juniper is a native pine, which was once widespread in the wild but today is largely restricted to areas of the Scottish Highlands and the chalk lands of southern England. An oil distilled from its berries is used to flavour gin – unsurprisingly, both the tree's leaves and bark smell of gin! Its dense growth provides shelter for nesting birds such as the firecrest, and it is a food plant for the caterpillars of a number of moth species. Changing land management practices, a liking for the leaves by rabbits and deer and the tree's slow-growing nature means the tree's range and numbers have declined in recent years.

THE YEW IS an incredibly long-living tree, easily reaching 500 years old: nearly a dozen trees in Britain are estimated at more than 1,000 years old. When exploring old village churchyards you will frequently come across yews planted there. This is thought to be to do with the tree's association with places of worship by ancient Britons, pre-Christianity – evidently some hundreds of churchyards have yew trees that are older than their churches. The yew was also seen as a symbol of immortality, being an evergreen. Unusual for a conifer, the yew bears its seeds not in a cone but in a fleshy berry. This is much liked by birds such as the mistle thrush and blackbird, as well as by squirrels and dormice.

INTRODUCED IN THE Middle Ages, the sycamore has naturalised across much of Britain. Although related to the maples, the widely lobed leaves are similar to those of the plane: the sycamore's botanical name, *Acer pseudoplatanus*, means 'like a plane tree'. Winged seed capsules helicopter in spirals to the ground in autumn.

Landscape and Culture

To TRAVEL THROUGH the countryside is to travel through time. The many marks on the landscape point to the thousands of years of habitation. Dating back through the Iron and Bronze Ages to the Stone Age are ancient burial mounds, hill figures, standing stones, forts, settlement sites and more.

NUMEROUS BURIAL MOUNDS known as barrows can be found throughout Britain, although most are concentrated in a swathe of upland between Dorset and eastern Yorkshire. Created for the burial of a community's chief and their family, the barrows date to the Neolithic period between 4000 and 2500 BC. Some early period long barrows (rectangular earth mounds) are as much as 91 m long, 30 m wide, and rise to about 4 m high. Barrows may be marked as 'tumuli' on maps, from the Latin *'tumere'*, meaning 'to swell'.

HUNDREDS OF ANCIENT standing stones are found across Britain, often formed into circles. They date to about 3000 BC. The most famous is of course Stonehenge in Wiltshire. Such stone circles are thought to have been gathering places for religious rites and to mark the coming and going of the seasons. Other 'should-see' circles include Avebury, also in Wiltshire, and the Rollright Stones in Oxfordshire.

THE YOUNGEST OF the prehistoric remains are hilltop forts that date from the Iron Age, back to about 1000 BC. There are literally thousands of these across Britain;

defensive structures that incorporate ditches and banks with sometimes walls built on top of the banks as a further defence. They are considered not to have been permanent settlements but more likely temporary sites for use in times of trouble.

ON THE CHALK hills throughout England are a number of giant-sized hill figures cut into the earth and visible for miles around. Some are relatively modern – only hundreds of years old – but the most famous and undoubtedly prehistoric is the Uffington White Horse in Oxfordshire, which may be as much as 4,000 years old. At 110 m long, the figure of the horse is formed from deep trenches filled with crushed white chalk. Situated on the upper slopes of White Horse Hill, it is best viewed from across the Vale of White Horse from the villages of Longcot, Great Coxwell and Fernham.

OTHER HILL FIGURES cut into hillsides in addition to the famous Uffington Horse feature both horses and human figures. Many more are thought to have disappeared over the centuries. Of those still to be seen, none are as old as the Uffington Horse – they're more likely to be hundreds of years old rather than thousands, and include:

THE CERNE ABBAS Giant – the depiction of a giant naked man (55 m high) with what has been described as a 'substantial' erect penis (it is 11 m long), which makes this one memorable. It is carved into the side of a hill near the village of Cerne Abbas in Dorset. Its origins are a mystery but it is thought to be no older than the seventeenth century.

THE LONG MAN of Wilmington – at
69-m high, this can be seen on one of the slopes of
Windover Hill near Eastbourne. Again, most probably
seventeenth century and origins unknown.

THERE ARE SOME 15 other white horse figures and at
least fifty landscape figures in total around Britain,
most of them in Wiltshire.

A LINGERING PERIOD of unseasonable heat and
sunshine in late autumn, when although summer has
faded, warmth and leaves lingered on, is commonly
called an Indian summer, from the American usage.
However in Britain in former days such a period of
weather was known as a St Martin's summer, referring
to the feast-day of St Martin on 11 November,
or alternately a St Luke's little summer when the
unusually summery days occurred around St Luke's
day on 18 October.

Tips

MANY NEOLITHIC BARROWS – burial mounds – are open to the public and worth taking the time to see, as being among the oldest monuments and structures in Britain they provide a tangible starting point to our history. You can see long barrows at:

SUTTON HOO, SUFFOLK
One of the most famous Anglo-Saxon burial sites, the area is dotted with burial mounds, some of which are thought to be those of old warriors.

STONEY LITTLETON LONG BARROW, SOMERSET
A smaller tomb at about 30-m long, but again with side chambers which can be viewed.

STREET HOUSE LONG BARROW, NORTH YORKSHIRE
Only partial remains of the barrow can still be seen, although outlines in the ground and parts of stone walls are also visible. The original structure is thought to have been an early Neolithic cairn that was later overlaid by a Bronze Age burial mound.

PIPTON LONG BARROW, POWYS
An even smaller barrow with little remaining above ground, but thought to cover burial chambers below ground. This barrow is on private land and permission must be sought to visit it.

West Kennet Long Barrow, Wiltshire
In Avebury, near the stone circles. West Kennet is
one of the best-preserved and most impressive long
barrows – it is over 100 m in length. The chambered
tomb sheltered the remains of numerous people of
the time.

Wayland's Smithy, Oxfordshire
Another chambered burrow dating to 3590 BC, and
a double barrow in fact, the top mound was added
100–200 years after its first construction.

FOR THE COUNTRYSIDE'S mammals autumn isn't all
about feeding up ahead of winter – for deer it's also
a time of sorting out territory and mating. While
the female deer group into herds, the biggest males
stake out their right to mate with them in noisy
displays of strength and size that can also involve
clashing fights between competing males. This, the
annual rut, or roar, takes place through October to
early November and if you're lucky you can get to
witness this in the raw. Places where you might see
the rut include: Epping Forest in Greater London;
the Forest of Dean in Gloucestershire; and Thetford
Forest in Norfolk; and those places with parkland
herds such as Richmond Park and Bushy Park, both
in Greater London; Calke Abbey in Derbyshire;
Petworth House and Park in West Sussex; Woburn
Abbey in Bedfordshire; and Knole Park in Kent. You
need to get there early in the morning to
see the rutting.

Notes

1
....

2
....

3
....

4
....

5
....

6
....

7
....

8
....

9
....

10
....

11
....

12
....

13
....

14
....

15 ....

16 ....

17 ....

18 ....

19 ....

20 ....

21 ....

22 ....

23 ....

24 ....

25 ....

26 ....

27 ....

28 ....

29 ....

30 ....

31 ....

November

LATE AUTUMN. *A month for fog and frosts – frosts that will strip deciduous trees bare of any remaining leaves. Already the air holds a wonderful earth scent from leaves that have fallen and are beginning to moulder. Meanwhile, bracken and bramble continue to provide a richness of colour to countryside walks with tints of gold and purple-brown. On farms there will be tending to winter wheat, and the laying of new hedges will be underway now that hedge tree species are free of leaves.*

Wildlife

A GROUP OF small birds with a flitting flight, the tits include the familiar and well-loved blue tit along with a handful of other species. The willow tit is another smartly turned out member of the group, with a black cap to its head, black bib and white cheeks. Body plumage is brown on upper parts, buff-grey on underparts, but it can be very difficult to tell this one apart from the marsh tit – ornithologists didn't separate the two until just a hundred years ago. Willow tits are found in thickets in damp areas by bogs and marshes and can be told apart from marsh tits by their distinctive 'pitchoo' call.

THE LONG-TAILED TIT is a representative of a different family to the common tits but is gregarious and commonly associates with them. Now, in winter, the long-tailed tit can be seen flocking with others in their search for insects and late autumn seeds. The long-tailed tit is easily recognisable in its unusual pink and black colouring and long tail.

OF THE THREE swans in Britain, the mute swan is the most usually seen, and the only one resident. It is readily distinguished from the others, which are also white, by the elegant, curved way in which the mute swan holds its neck. The whooper swan and Bewick's swan visit from autumn to spring, the former from Iceland and the latter from its home in Siberia. Bewick's swan is similar to the whooper but smaller – and both hold their necks straight and upright. By law the Queen has a right to all of Britain's mute swans but in practice only exercises this right along the stretch of the River Thames. Until recent times the illegal killing of a mute swan was an act of treason.

THE CONFLICT OVER Britain's two squirrel species illustrates with awful clarity the impact introduced species can have on native wildlife, in this case between the eastern grey squirrel, introduced here from America in the 1870s, and the red squirrel, a native since prehistoric times. A larger, stronger animal and an aggressive adapter, the grey squirrel has largely displaced the red squirrel from its traditional feeding territories and has become vastly more numerous. It's estimated that today there are only some 140,000 red squirrels left, confined to parts of northern England and on the Isle of Wight in the south; the grey squirrel on the other hand numbers around 2.5 million.

THE RED SQUIRREL is more limited in its diet than the grey, favouring the seeds of conifers, but also eating nuts, berries and fungi. It spends much of its life high up in conifer forests, favouring pine cones but also eating spruce and larch. They do not hibernate and must store food to help them get through winter. They build a balled-up nest, or drey, of grass, twigs, leaves and bark in the forks or hollows of trees. Grey squirrels prefer foraging on the ground and have a more diverse diet, and are found in greater concentrations in woodland than red squirrels.

Field and Flower

INTRODUCED TO BRITAIN in the seventeenth century, the larch is one of those unusual conifers that is not evergreen – its needles yellow in autumn and then drop. It is identifiable by its graceful form and small cones that are held upright. Its introduction was initially as an ornamental species but the larch came to be extensively planted when the value of its timber was realised, along with an appreciation of its quick growth and ability to withstand subfreezing temperatures. Its seeds are sought out by various birds as well as red squirrels.

THE SILVER BIRCH and the very similar downy birch are both native trees and identified by the white bark on the trunks and drooping branches of small diamond-shaped light green leaves. These dance and turn prettily in a breeze and will have turned golden-brown in autumn. Birch is a hardy species, a first coloniser of open ground. It thrives in the northern parts of Britain and in its mountains. The trunks are often drilled into by woodpeckers making nesting holes.

THE ENGLISH HOLLY with its shiny green spiked leaves and bright red berries provides a welcome shot of colour and presence in this month's often monochromatic days. Commonly found in the understory of beech and oak woodlands (it is very shade-tolerant) it will grow to about 15 m. While the prickled leaves are a defence against browsing (though conversely the leaves and the holly's dense growth creates ideal protected nesting spots for birds) as trees age and as the browsing height is surpassed perhaps, leaves are more likely to be smooth. The red berries are eaten by birds and by the likes of dormice and wood mice. Often seen in old hedgerows, holly was also in past times one of the trees used as a marker tree for boundaries such as parish boundaries.

THE ELDER GROWS in woodland and in hedgerows. A smallish tree, it has been much surrounded by superstition through the years: plant an elder by your house, it is said, and you'll keep evil witches away. The creamy, highly scented flowers appear as large flat umbels that are followed by purplish-black berries. Both flowers and berries are used in myriad ways including for wine, cordial, jams and chutneys, the flower umbels dipped in batter and fried, the berries cooked up with other fruits. Because the berries are preferential for badgers, badger setts are often found in the vicinity of elder trees.

Landscape and Culture

FOR MANY PEOPLE, the countryside village is an idyll, nestled in the countryside among farms, far from the madding crowd. And many do retain these qualities despite others having been subsumed by nearby towns, or becoming dormitory areas and as a consequence losing their economic infrastructure. Typically the traditional village has a population between a few hundred and a few thousand and has shops, a pub and a church: historically the distinction between a village and the smaller hamlet was the presence of a church.

OVER THE CENTURIES a great many villages have disappeared from the map, sometimes leaving a ruined church behind, but often as not little trace is left apart from undulations in the fields. Deserted medieval villages number in their thousands. Sometimes the reasons were depopulation, economic shifts, and the Black Death of the fourteenth century is also held to have precipitated the collapse of a number of such villages. The enclosures of the fifteenth and sixteenth centuries led to villages all over Britain being abandoned.

THE DESERTED VILLAGE of Wharram Percy in North Yorkshire is the best-known example of a village brought down by economic shift, when in the fifteenth century the cereal-growing that had employed so many of its residents gave way to pastoral farming. Eventually the last remaining families were forced out by the local lord of the manor and the houses taken down to accommodate more grazing land. Its ruined church is still there, and the village's layout is still visible in the area surrounding.

POLLARDING IS A common pruning system used on trees in hedgerows and elsewhere, whereby the upper branches are cut off to force a dense head of regrowth branches that can be used for timber and fuel. Use is also made of the foliage as stock feed. Pollarding differs from coppicing in that coppicing is done at ground level while pollarding is above head height. ('Poll' is an old word for the top of the head; 'to poll' meant 'to cut the hair' and this is also seen with 'polled' cattle which have had their horns removed.) Trees that make effective pollards are planes, beeches, hornbeams and yews.

HERDS OF WILD ponies have been a majestic feature of wild areas of the country for many hundreds of years – the wild ponies of the New Forest may have been there for as long as 2,000 years. Exmoor and Dartmoor also have their own wild herds and there are fell ponies in Wales as well. While these animals can trace their origin to prehistoric ponies, they are not true wild populations but largely previously domesticated animals, now running semi-feral. It is thought a handful of true wild ponies may still be found in very out-of-the-way corners of the Scottish islands or high in the mountains of Wales.

Tips

THIS IS THE month that red squirrels are in preparation mode for winter, feeding up to improve their condition against the paucity of food over winter and storing up nuts and other food. Although a rarity in Britain, you can see them in the wild at a number of places, including special sanctuaries that have been established to help them prosper in the face of the more assertive grey squirrel. Three quarters of Britain's red squirrel population is in Scotland.

SCOTLAND
Dalbeattie Forest, Dumfries and Galloway
Balloch Wood, Dumfries and Galloway
Eskrigg Nature Reserve, Lockerbie
Galloway Forest Park, Dumfries and Galloway
Mabie Forest, Dumfries and Galloway
Hyndlee Forest, Scottish Borders
Craik Forest, Scottish Borders
Atholl Estates, Perth and Kinross

ENGLAND
Whinlatter Forest Park, Cumbria
Robin Hill Country Park, Isle of Wight
Parkhurst Forest, Isle of Wight
Kielder Forest, Northumberland
Brownsea Island, Dorset
Greenfield Forest, Yorkshire
Escot Estate, Devon

Not that one needs a purpose – just being in the countryside is a tonic in itself – but there are a number of 'themed' walks one can do that adds to the enjoyment. For instance, why not combine a wee dram with a wander on a very pleasant walk through Scottish countryside between two of the region's great whiskey makers – from Scotland's smallest distillery, Edradour, then on to one of its oldest, Blair Athol. On the way you get to pass woods and a stream, grain fields, glimpse deer, and enjoy mountain views. Yellow waymarkers will help guide you there.

Notes

1
....

2
....

3
....

4
....

5
....

6
....

7
....

8
....

9
....

10
....

11
....

12
....

13
....

14
....

15

16

17

18

19

20

21

22

23

24

25

26

27

28

29

30

December

EARLY WINTER. DAYS are short and the shadows long. There is beauty in the bare forms of trees and the cold silence. Wild berries are important to the countryside's birds and some of the non-hibernating mammals and cutting of hedgerows will usually be delayed until this food resource has been eaten. On the farm, dairy cows will have been brought inside barns now, while beef cattle may remain outside at grass while there is still growth. Sheep will graze as best they can, receiving supplementary feed in poor weather.

Wildlife

THE NUTHATCH IS a small woodland bird
noticeable for its head-down aspect when
descending tree trunks. Colouring is blue-grey
on upper parts, pink-brown on breast and belly
and with a stripe on the side of its head that passes
across the eye. Nests are made in holes in the trunks
of trees, or in old nests once used by woodpeckers.
To ensure its nest is protected against larger birds,
the nuthatch uses mud to plaster around the entrance
to the nest, reducing the size of the hole so only the
nuthatch can use it.

THE TREECREEPER IS another small, active woodland
bird that feeds on insects on the bark of tree trunks
and branches using its long curved beak to extricate
insects. Its upper body is brown, the underparts white.
Above the eye is a white stripe. Its foraging method
is distinctive as it works its way up a tree trunk in a
spiral (as opposed to the nuthatch that moves *down*
the tree). Nest sites are frequently constructed in the
gap behind a branch or a piece of bark that has been
forced away from the trunk.

THE FIVE SPECIES of grouse in Britain make their home on upland areas, heather moorlands and open woodlands. The black grouse and the capercaillie both have very small populations and are considered at risk in Britain. The red grouse is the most populous and is common on heather moors in most upland parts. It is descended from the willow grouse, which still lives in western regions of Scotland, Ireland and Wales. The ptarmigan is confined to the cold uplands and mountains of Scotland. In winter its plumage changes to pure white, while feathers grow over its feet to provide insulation from the cold. Come spring the white plumage reverts to a patchy mix of brown and grey-flecked white.

COMMONLY SEEN, WEASELS, stoats and ferrets are members of the family of carnivorous mustelids. The ferret, smallest of the three (about 50 cm including tail) is a form of polecat. In past times it was domesticated for use in hunting rabbits and rats. Larger is the weasel (about 20 cm including tail) then larger still is the stoat (30 cm). In the north of Britain the stoat's coat turns a camouflage white in winter, and in this colouring it is known as ermine. Britain's mustelids, which also include the polecat, mink, otter and badger, are mainly nocturnal but are often seen during the day.

Field and Flower

AT THIS TIME of year mistletoe will be more visible in the tops of deciduous trees. Poplars and lime trees are typical host trees, as are apple trees in orchards. The mistletoe is a hemiparasite, deriving part of its nutrients from the bark of host trees to which it attaches itself. The pearl-like white berries appearing now are a lovely fit with the mid-green leaves. The plant's association with festivities in this season is considered to pre-date Christianity, a hold-over from ancient solstice traditions when evergreen plants in winter were seen as symbolising continuing life in the darkest of seasons. The custom of kissing under the mistletoe at Christmas is said to originate with the Ancient Greeks, but stories of its origins in other cultures abound.

CONIFERS OF THE countryside comprise a large group of trees that includes spruces, yews and firs, pines, cedars and larches, hemlocks, cypresses and thuja. Most have been introduced from Europe and North America; native are the juniper, yew and the Scots pine.

THE SCOTS PINE is recognised by its straight trunk, scaly orange-brown bark, blue-green needles and the flat or rounded shape of the tree's crown. It grows to about 35 m and is found in the Scottish Highlands in remnants of the Caledonian Forest, an ancient forest in Scotland. The floor of these forests is often covered with heather and bracken. Unlike the forests of the introduced conifers that are generally low on associated wildlife, a number of birds and mammals make their homes within forests of Scots pine.

THE ROWAN IS notable for the masses of red-orange berries they produce in autumn, often still apparent in December, which are targeted by birds, the blackbird in particular. Rowan trees are common in the wild, particularly in the Scottish highlands. It is also known as mountain ash for the similarity of its leaves to the common ash, but the two species are not related.

ON FARMS, WHEN conditions are dry, farmers will look to do some early ploughing in order to allow as long a period as possible over winter for frosts to break down the soil and reduce the need for extra machine cultivation which would increase the risk of compacting the earth. Hard frosts are effective in breaking up clods and help to produce a friable ground for spring crops. Winter wheat is Britain's most widely grown cereal crop, with about twice the amount of barley and as much as twenty times the amount of oats grown.

Landscape and Culture

REVERENCE FOR TREES in European culture derives from pre-Christian times when trees – the greatest living things in the landscape and providers of food, fuel and building materials for shelter – were unsurprisingly seen as eminent in life. Forests were sacred places. Those who came to Britain to convert its people to Christianity saw worshipping trees as idolatry but, being pragmatic, recognised the opportunity for grafting the new religion onto the stock of existing beliefs. Hence early Christians built churches near sites of pagan worship in forest glades, in order that the new religion might more easily be grafted onto customs such as winter solstice celebrations.

TREES, AND THE countryside in which they stand, continue to have a special place in the hearts of Britons, and of the millions of visitors to Britain as well. The countryside is simply unique. Charming, human-scaled, a mix of the natural and the domesticated. No matter how much it is idealised – the villages, the prettiness of country lanes and hedgerows, the magnificent landscape views, the fields and trees and hills – the attraction of the British countryside makes a real claim on most hearts. It's an attraction that has been reflected in poetry through the ages:

> Happy the man whose wish and care
> A few paternal acres bound,
> Content to breathe his native air
> In his own ground.

December

Whose herds with milk, whose fields with bread,
Whose flocks supply him with attire;
Whose trees in summer yield him shade,
In winter fire.

From 'The Quiet Life' by Alexander Pope

A ripple of land; such little hills, the sky
Can stoop to tenderly and the wheatfields climb;
Such nooks of valleys, lined with orchises,
Fed full of noises by invisible streams;
And open pastures, where you scarcely tell
White daisies from white dew, – at intervals
The mythic oaks and elm-trees standing out
Self-poised upon their prodigy of shade, –
I thought my father's land was worthy too
Of being my Shakespeare's…
I flattered all the beauteous country round,
As poets use… the skies, the clouds, the fields,
The happy violets hiding from the roads
The primroses run down to, carrying gold –
The tangled hedgerows, where the cows push out
Impatient horns and tolerant churning mouths
'Twixt dripping ash-boughs – hedgerows all alive
With birds and gnats and large white butterflies
Which look as if the May-flower had sought life
And palpitated forth upon the wind –
Hills, vales, woods, netted in a silver mist,
Farm, granges, doubled up among the hills,
And cattle grazing in the watered vales,
And cottage-chimneys smoking from the woods,
And cottage-gardens smelling everywhere,
Confused with smell of orchards.

From Aurora Leigh by Elizabeth Barrett Browning

Tips

WINTER WALKS THIS month can be
put to good use by collecting odd bits of
greenery here and there – pieces of fir, ivy and
holly leaves and berries, for making into a Christmas
wreath. Such evergreenery was part of pre-Christian
winter solstice celebrations marking the start of the
lengthening days and the approach of spring. 'Wreath'
derives from the Old English 'writha', whose meaning
is to twist. Be considerate with your 'pruning' though
to make sure you leave your gathering spot unharmed.

BRITAIN IS A land of castles and you're never far
from one to visit. Ruined though some may be it
detracts nothing from their presence and majesty.
Scotland, Northumberland and Wales are particularly
well represented with castles but you'll find them
everywhere across the countryside. Here's a selection
of some of the finest:

Dunstanburgh Castle, Northumberland
Eilean Donan Castle, Western Highlands, Scotland
Arundel Castle, West Sussex
Restormel Castle, Cornwall
Okehampton Castle, Devon
Carrickfergus Castle, Northern Ireland
Urquhart Castle, Inverness, Scotland
Orford Castle, Suffolk
Conwy, Harlech, Beaumaris, Denbigh, Ewloe and
Criccieth castles – all in Wales

On the sticky matter of telling crows apart, a
countryside rule of thumb goes as follows:

'A crow in a crowd is a rook
A rook on its own is a crow.'

Notes

1 ....

2 ....

3 ....

4 ....

5 ....

6 ....

7 ....

8 ....

9 ....

10 ....

11 ....

12 ....

13 ....

14 ....

December

15
....

16
....

17
....

18
....

19
....

20
....

21
....

22
....

23
....

24
....

25
....

26
....

27
....

28
....

29
....

30
....

31
....

Index

The
Seaside
Year

Isobel Carlson

THE SEASIDE YEAR

Isobel Carlson

ISBN: 978 1 84953 697 4

Hardback

£9.99

This charming and practical handbook is bursting with tips, facts and folklore to guide you through a year by the sea. Find out how to identify shells by shape and markings, choose the best coastal routes to explore and learn about the geography of the beautiful beaches and craggy cliffs that Great Britain has to offer.

With handy diary pages for making your own notes each month, this is a must-have for any eager seaside explorer.

THE WALKER'S YEAR

David Bathurst

ISBN: 978 1 84953 696 7

Hardback

£9.99

This charming and practical handbook is bursting with tips, facts and folklore to guide those who love to roam through the natural rhythms and seasons of the year. Find out how to identify flora by colour and shape, discover routes of outstanding natural beauty and learn about the diverse wildlife that can be found across Britain. Also includes useful notes pages for documenting your exploration of countryside, shore, cliffs and forests. A must-have for any lover of the great outdoors!

The
Birdwatcher's
Year

Richard
Williamson

THE BIRDWATCHER'S YEAR

Richard Williamson

ISBN: 978 1 84953 436 9

Hardback

£9.99

This charming and practical handbook is bursting with tips, facts and folklore to guide you through the birdwatching year. Find out how to identify birds by sight or song, everything you need to know about their behaviour, habitats and breeding and migration habits, and tips for encouraging birds into your garden. Also includes handy diary pages for making your own notes each month. A must-have for any eager birdwatcher.

'Enchanting and knowledgeable'
                    THE SIMPLE THINGS magazine

'Packed with anecdotes and tips, it is an instructive read'
                    THE GOOD BOOK GUIDE

If you're interested in finding out more about our books, find us on Facebook at **Summersdale Publishers** and follow us on Twitter at **@Summersdale**.

www.summersdale.com